# HEAL
## Healthy Emotions. Abundant Life.

*From Super Hero to Super Self-Empowerment*

*Master your Emotional Intelligence*

Cynthia Howard RN, CNC, PhD

Praise for HEAL

*HEAL helps you get unstuck and love yourself more!*

*Knowing and loving yourself is the key to getting beyond what stops you from moving ahead. HEAL provides you with the tools to discover who you are and why you have been doing the same thing over and over again. Whether it is an emotional reaction to a certain situation or an immediate grab for some candy to feel better, it is all within you ready to be released. Let Dr. Cynthia help you get unstuck and love yourself more with her easy to follow tools in HEAL: Healthy Emotions. Abundant Life. You will thank yourself!*

—Anne Salisbury, PhD, ThD, MA, MBA

*I only wish I would have had Dr. Cynthia's book when I started my career! Today it is common knowledge that mastering emotional intelligence is critical in advancing your career. More importantly, it is how this self-awareness will improve your life and your relationships. I read the entire book with interest but found the section on Boundaries to be especially meaningful and helpful to me. When meeting Cynthia in person I could hear her command of the subject matter and feel her generosity of spirit. Cynthia's book and coaching gently guides you through a process of understanding your emotions and empowers you to know how to handle and benefit from the emotions that serve us.*

—Michelle Podlesni, President,
National Nurses in Business Association

*HEAL has helped me understand my emotions and be able to love myself a little more. I am a recovering perfectionist. I can now laugh at myself.*

—Jessie Evans
Therapeutic Massage Therapist

*As a teacher of 15 years, I know how easy it is to fall into a state of burnout after years of caring for small children. You become so wrapped up in your role of caregiver that you fall into a routine of always thinking about your students' needs that you get lost and forget who you are . . .*

—Pat Lucas
Retired Educator

*This book is an eye-opening encounter with the daily stresses of life, stresses that tend to get swept under the rug or pushed aside... Dr. Cynthia offers a different approach: healing that comes from consistent, daily choices towards personal empowerment and self-care.*

—Callie Revell
Writer, Editor, Entrepreneur

*Dr. Cynthia helped me recognize the power of emotions. I had been avoiding them and stuffing them down with food. I am now confident about losing weight because I know I will not yo-yo anymore. I have a way out and feel so blessed by this book.*

—Carly Hinkle
Organizer, Mom

*I have always felt like a fake. I work harder than anyone and still never felt like anything I did was good enough. Now I know this is not true. I look forward to accepting myself more.*

—Robyn Strand
RN, BSN, Critical Care


*Thank you for writing this. I can see now, I have been acting out the theme my family wanted for me. As the oldest of the oldest, I was supposed to take care of my family. I resented that. I do not want to be a martyr. I now have a way through this.*

—Cecie W.
Teacher


*This book helped me cool down my anger. I was exhausted from being angry all the time.*

—Roberta Frank
Customer Service

Copyright © 2015, 2016 Cynthia Howard RN, CNC, PhD
All rights reserved. No part of this book may be reproduced or transmitted in any form or by any means, electronic or mechanical, including photocopying, recording or by any information storage and retrieval system without written permission of the publisher, except for the inclusion of brief quotations in a review.

Printed in the United States of America

Cynthia Howard RN, CNC, PhD

HEAL: Healthy Emotions. Abundant Life.
ISBN: 978-0-9907977-0-8
Cover design by Todd Siatkowsky, Special Forces Art Department

DISCLAIMER
This book is designed to provide information on emotions, emotional intelligence, resilience and mindfulness. It is sold with the understanding that the publisher and author are not engaged in rendering medical, counseling, or other professional services. If counseling or other expert assistance is required, the services of a specialist should be sought.

The purpose of this manual is to educate and inspire. The author and publisher shall have neither liability nor responsibility to any person or entity with respect to any loss or damage caused, or alleged to have been caused, directly or indirectly, by the information contained in this book.

# TABLE OF CONTENTS

HOW THIS BOOK CAN CHANGE YOUR LIFE .......................................... 2

TIMELESS PATTERNS AND THE MYTHS WE LIVE BY ..................... 13

THE SUPERHERO AND THE IMPOSTER SYNDROME ........................ 41

WHY IS EMOTIONAL INTELLIGENCE SO IMPORTANT? ................... 48

BURNED OUT TO BRILLIANT ................................................................. 55

RESILIENCE: PATH TO TRUE HAPPINESS ........................................... 61

YOUR BODY TALKS: ARE YOU LISTENING? ........................................ 68

UNDERSTANDING EMOTIONS ................................................................ 74

EMOTIONS AS GUIDES: WHAT THEY ARE TRYING TO TELL YOU ................................................................................................................ 84

YOU ARE MORE THAN YOUR EMOTIONS ........................................... 121

YOUR SUPERPOWERS ........................................................................... 134

LIFE IN FLOW ........................................................................................... 152

WAYS WE CAN WORK TOGETHER ...................................................... 153

ABOUT THE AUTHOR .............................................................................. 154

"The privilege of a lifetime is being
who you are . . ."

—Joseph Campbell

# Acknowledgements

Gratitude is really food for the soul. I hope that you will have greater appreciation for yourself, your struggles, and your potential as a result of this book. Thank *you* for wanting more for yourself. This is what changes the world.

I am very grateful for the many people I have worked with who allowed me to join them in their most important undertaking—mastering their own lives. It was indeed a privilege and honor to serve you as you slayed your inner dragons blocking your success.

This journey we took together showed me that embracing the struggle is always worth the effort; you emerge transformed, renewed, and ready to live life your own way. This is the nature of abundance.

I thank my intuition—a.k.a. my Inner Genius—for the guidance and direction to write this book.

My deepest gratitude is to the grace and love of God as I travel my own journey beyond the myth of who I thought I was to the truth of an exceptionally full life.

*I came that they may have life and have it abundantly.*
*(John 10:10)*

# HOW THIS BOOK CAN CHANGE YOUR LIFE

Most people know when they are hungry, cold, or tired and take the steps to protect themselves from any harm. Yet, few successfully manage the emotional challenges that can take down one's life if not addressed. It is this emotional clarity that also allows you to live abundantly, which I define as the ability to do what you want when you want to. This book is a toolkit for emotional awareness for better relationships, more lucrative opportunities, and greater fulfillment as a human being.

Starting with our first breath, we knew how to get someone's attention: we cried. Life started out fairly simple; if we were hungry, cold, tired, or cranky, we cried—and we usually got the results we wanted. In order to learn about ourselves, we relied on other people. If we were loved, we felt loved; if we weren't, we thought it was our fault and made up a story about that. Before long, that story became "just the way it is," and life followed a pattern that was established before we could even talk. Without knowing it, you can end up living life based on those early stories and treating yourself the way you were treated. And this is a problem.

Do you really want to live your life looking through someone else's filter? We build our self-worth based on someone else's opinion. Even if it is from someone you may love, like your parents, it is based on their views of life. As you grow, your uniqueness will challenge those early beliefs, others' held about you, and push you beyond your comfort zone.

The earliest beliefs about yourself are not automatically updated with the many new experiences you have in the course of your life. The early stories (and beliefs) about you stay the motivating driver behind your choices, large and small, until you challenge them. Most of the time, there is a wake-up call that shakes up your life and forces you to re-evaluate everything. Even when your foundation is challenged, you have the option to continue believing the old story; think twice, if your life is not going as you want it to, then this can be the beginning of a new chapter.

I will be talking about the timeless stories that can get played out in life that short-change one's fullest expression of who they are: the story of the Rebel Without a Cause, the Orphan, the Caregiver, the Superhero, and others. Each character provides a lesson and a gift for you when you embrace their messages.

We are all unique and blessed with a set of gifts and talents, and we all yearn to be loved and seen for who we really are. Too often, we believe we have to buy this love by doing what we think someone else wants. You may have already figured out, that trying too hard to be loved, gets in the way of getting it. What if you could take all that energy spent in chasing happiness, pleasing other people, and looking for love and acceptance in all the wrong places and finally learn to love and accept yourself—just as you are right now?

It may seem like too big of a challenge—to love yourself now, without reservation, when you still have so much about yourself you don't like. After all, you are so imperfect. Most people are taught to focus on their weaknesses and keep striving to be better. And yes, of course, we all want to be better human beings. The way to the top of this mountain is to love you first. Are you thinking, "I can only love myself once I lose the weight, graduate from school, make my first million, get married, have the child, finally stop smoking," and on and on and on? "If I settle and accept how I am now, I won't be motivated to change, right?"

*How is that working for you?*

The relief from this endless struggle comes the very moment you give up trying to *be* something and you simply *live fully* in the moment. The point of your power lies in the present moment. This is all the time you really have, and your power comes from living truthfully. If you stopped right now and accepted that you are a magnificent being capable of whatever you choose to do, how would that feel?

*What would you attempt to do if you believed in yourself?*

The sooner you learn to love yourself—as is—the sooner you will stop the struggle (and any sabotage) and move forward in your life. This is the wake-up call to transform one moment into great possibility.

Have you been thinking about going back to school, opening a business, beginning a new relationship, running a marathon, starting a family, or ending a marriage but feel afraid, doubt yourself, or dismiss it entirely? Would you like to implement some work-life balance without all the guilt?

Being stuck can last years. The resistance you feel becomes a new normal. Being stuck can become an identity.

Nothing will ever change, right? So, why bother to take that class or learn accounting for your business? Why go to the gym? It's no use; your relationship will never change. And deep inside, you may not know how to change yourself. It becomes easy to simply complain about your life and the lack of opportunity. Deep inside, a part of you knows you are giving up; it is easier than continuing to feel that fear.

Maybe you are ready to move forward, but you have so much emotional baggage and do not know how to let it all go. Or, you could have trouble saying no and are stuck in the caregiver role. Are you a superhero taking on too much without any time for yourself? Is it hard to say what you mean, and are you burning up about it? Has Tums become your only relief?

I have worked with thousands of people in my twenty-plus years of running a private coaching practice, and I have helped amazing people move beyond trauma, abuse, self-doubt, emotional baggage, and other barriers to live exceptional lives. I wrote this book to provide inspiration and a map for *your* transformation.

Too many people live with internal conflict, unaware of the drain this is and the limitations it creates in their lives. They are not aware of the power they have to change their relationships to themselves and how this will change the outcome of their lives. Life is filled with challenges—some real, most imagined. The truth is, most of the difficulty experienced on a daily basis comes from the scenarios played out in one's own mind, most of which never happen.

What if you could harness this innate power and live in sync with your desires? This book will help you live with less conflict and have more of what you want. Life is meant to be an adventure we live, not something to coast through. Learning is part of that ride. HEAL will help you with the most important piece of this adventure—learning about yourself.

Someone in one of my workshops said to me, "Do you really believe someone can change just like that?" The short answer is, "Yes," and the long answer is, "It depends on what you believe." This book is the beginning of a journey you can take to break through your barriers to an abundant life. Would you like your life to be easier? You can stop chasing the answer; it doesn't live in the next job, relationship, weight loss, or lottery ticket. It is inside of you. The very thing you have been avoiding holds the answer to your transformation.

Of the clients who came to me saying they think nothing will ever change, ninety-eight percent left and abandoned that belief, filled with new hope of possibility for themselves. Having worked with thousands of people, this seems like a good track record. I want you to have the opportunity to move beyond your barriers and embrace a more abundant life. You have the answers inside; I provide the keys to access it.

I did not always believe this myself. I have limited myself with fears and self-doubt, and I have been through periods of self-sabotage. Early in my nursing career, I asked these questions:

"Is aging really the answer to why people have low energy and health problems?"

"Why is diet and lifestyle so hard to correct?"

"Why do some people achieve success and others don't?"

"Is life something you have to accept 'as is,' or can you control your destiny?"

These questions drove me to graduate school where I studied stress, burnout, and why some people flourish and others do not. I remembered the diabetic patient who could not stop eating sugar even though it was literally killing her. I thought about myself: I was smoking cigarettes when, as a nurse, I fully knew the health risks. I thought about my colleagues who, as healthcare professionals, did not take care of themselves and pushed and pushed until they hit the wall. Too many of my colleagues were using coffee like it was a drug and then taking sleeping pills and antidepressants to balance "brain chemistry." This did not seem like the best solution because, in the end, they still were not happy or fulfilled.

*Is there a short answer to living a life that is happy, fulfilled, abundant, and easy? Can you really have it all?*

To get the most out of life, you have to go through the shadow side, so you can live a whole, complete, and fulfilled life. *HEAL: Healthy Emotions. Abundant Life.* is your toolkit for this journey. I wrote this book because healthy emotions and the message they provide for a fulfilled life are not talked about; instead, it is the damage emotions can cause that you hear about.

Toxic relationships, rage, anger, regret, and other emotional storms light up the blogs. Most of us do not learn how to take care of and learn from our emotions; they are treated like the black box in an airplane, only looked at when there has been a crash.

Emotions carry mixed messages, and most people would rather ignore them. This is a problem because, left alone, your emotions will wreak havoc in your life and with your health. Because emotions are acted out rather than identified, most people end up fearing the very inner resource that can empower them. Emotions and the message they have for you are the missing link in achieving the life you really want.

*How do you begin to name and claim your emotions when they have been buried for so long?*

This book provides an answer to these big questions. The tools and resources you need are buried underneath the emotional quicksand that comes from the patterns of over- and under-reacting. HEAL is your guide to go beyond the fear of the unknown and access the power in your emotions. It is time to recognize that emotions are part of your survival instinct and absolutely necessary for everyday life. Without access to your emotions, you could not make even simple decisions or enjoy simple pleasures.

*What does it cost you to keep that anger bottled up? Did you know you lose the ability to be happy in direct proportion to what you hold back?*

To move beyond the hijacking that happens when emotions are buried, you have to be willing to look at both sides of your emotion, the light side and shadow side. When you master this ability to know and care for yourself, you will master success. You will go from being closed off and shut down, driven by fear, to feeling energized by what is possible for you. You have a gift the world needs. There is no virtue in playing small.

As you go through the book, start a conversation with your deeper wisdom, those archetypal patterns and even the shadow; it will provide answers to so much confusion about why you do what you do. This is how the world changes—one person at a time. The ripple effect is actually very profound because as you change, so do all your relationships, and the chain reaction is set in motion. I can promise you that as you change, all your relationships will change. It will all be good.

As you open up to you, you will get underneath many of the mixed messages you have received about emotions to learn what is healthy, and how they can guide you. I will introduce five superpowers for that guilt-free work-life balance.

You will learn about emotional patterns that have kept you stuck, the stress reaction and risk for burnout, emotional intelligence, and how you can achieve true happiness. You will build awareness and wake up to what your body, mind, heart, and soul want you to know.

Your emotions are your GPS (Guide to Personal Success). Unfortunately, most of us have learned negative messages related to emotions, including:

- Emotions are irrational.
- One should keep them out of decisions and interactions.
- Or, better yet, you cannot trust your emotions.

The opposite of these assumptions is really true.

Emotions are integral to everything you do, and when you can embrace their guidance, you will enhance all relationships at work and at home. You will also explore what you previously learned about emotions and how this impacts your ability to relate to yourself and everyone else.

One of my simple definitions of emotions is "energy in motion." That is overly simplistic, I know. What it did for me was acknowledge that there are no good or bad emotions; they simply act as our messengers and instruct us to take some type of action, just like the warning lights on the dashboard of your car. I needed to have this balance for myself as I started to heal my own emotions.

Growing up in a proverbially dysfunctional home with parents vacillating between rage and silence, I learned emotions were dangerous. My early childhood conditioning taught me that emotions would do serious damage if they were unleashed. Later, I learned that emotions are designed to flow freely and inform us about everything going on around us.

*What did you learn about your emotions as a child? What is your relationship with them?*

Emotions are aspects of intelligence. They affect everything you do. They are an integral part of who you are, and—no matter how evolved you are—you just cannot separate yourself from your emotions. Emotions are not the enemy. I will talk about what neuroscience tells us about our emotions.

This book lays a foundation of emotional awareness, which I call Super Self-Empowerment. I am excited about the program and its potential to lead you to a more fulfilled life. Read on, reflect on the questions, step back from the emotional charge, and observe. As you engage this mindful approach, you will identify what is going on inside of you. This is not psychotherapy, and we are not going to specifically address trauma and abuse. I highly recommend engaging someone qualified to address these issues. I have resources in the back of this book.

This program will teach you to learn from your emotions, strengthen your intuition and your self-acceptance. Too many people have learned to ignore their emotions at their own peril.

*Have you hit a wall? Been stuck for years? Lost interest in life?*

This is what happens when emotions are trapped inside and have been buried; fear, self doubt and cynicism replace passion and purpose.

Today, healthy emotions are lost in lost in irritability, overwhelm, and stressed-out reactions. The word HEAL, as the title, has universal application. We all need healing on some level.

For some, there are obvious physical needs that show up as heart disease, diabetes, immune disorders, and cancer, to name a few. We are more than just our bodies. What crushed emotions might be underneath this physical process?

For others, there is a spiritual need for healing, as in the case of addictions. The obvious addictions to drugs, alcohol, sex, shopping, and food often have their origins in early childhood trauma, familial tendency, and shame. The less obvious addiction to sugar and junk food has its roots, in my opinion, in the lack of a heart-centered lifestyle and the reliance on a stressed-out nervous system to function under all the pressures of daily life. These addictions create physical and emotional issues, setting up a cascade effect and making it difficult for traditional medicine to effectively find solutions to health problems. How many prescriptions do you take before you start to ask the question, "What do I need to heal?"

The need for emotional healing is less obvious. If you start to listen to random conversations, you are likely to hear complaints, criticism, cynicism, despair, apathy, and boredom. Do you really think this pattern of thinking and interacting generates an abundant life?

Today, we live in what some would say is the best of times, with smart technology, gadgets, and apps to enhance everything we do. And yet, there is less awe, wonder, happiness, and joy, despite the great advancements in our world. I believe that most people today need emotional healing and would have more fulfilling lives if they were better tuned-in to the wisdom and guidance they have right inside of them.

As a little girl, I grew up in turmoil and confusion. I found that gazing at the stars at night was a way to ease the loneliness. Once, upon seeing a falling star, I had the experience of being connected to something bigger. Today, I know how fragile this connection can be; it takes effort and determination to preserve this childlike enthusiasm and wonder. Keep an open mind as you read this book.

*Heal: Healthy Emotions. Abundant Life.* is a program that will transform your relationship with yourself and elevate every other relationship you have, whether with friends, family, significant others, food, money, coworkers, God, success, or your dream.

This book weaves the stories of clients who have gone beyond their frustration, pain, and turmoil to finally enjoy the abundance that is theirs.

The book starts with stories of the universal and timeless characters called archetypes; the emotional metaphors that represent aspects of the self. We can all get stuck in an identity that is limiting. You will recognize yourself and others in these patterns and gain insight about how to move through them. This self-awareness is the foundation of emotional intelligence and crucial for success. At the end of the book, I present the Five Superpowers that will help you find your way to guilt-free work-life balance.

## HOW TO GET THE MOST FROM THIS BOOK

Be sure to jot down your thoughts, answer the questions, and take a moment to reflect. Write in the margins of the book, and let *you* come alive as you get closer to certain truths and insights that come up. This is your creative genius waking up.

Exercising your emotional intelligence means you are aware of what you are feeling, able to manage your emotions and still achieve your goals. As you go through this book, I'll help you understand how to move your emotions through your body, mind, heart, and soul for a more efficient way to learn from them.

Don't let the word "efficient" bother you. Most people spend way too much of their precious resources either holding emotions in or expressing them in a way that causes damage. Being efficient is not going to make you flat; it means that you will finally be in charge of what you are feeling and mindfully take the best action needed.

In this book, you will find:

- An introduction to the timeless patterns of behavior (archetypes); the characteristics, attitudes, and emotions that keep you stuck (and ultimately will set you free).
- Clarification on what emotions are and the purpose they serve.
- Guidelines to help you separate out healthy from unhealthy emotional expression.
- Exercises to integrate the splintered parts of yourself for a fulfilled life.
- Introduction to your energy system that is the source for your complete healing.
- How to have an exceptionally fulfilled life.

# CHAPTER 1

# TIMELESS PATTERNS AND THE MYTHS WE LIVE BY

*"Use the Force, Luke."*
—Obi-Wan Kenobi

Did you see the movie *Star Wars*? "May the force be with you"? This movie is one of my favorites. It combined great animation, action, and just the right amount of corny with the timeless story of transformation. Luke had to learn that he had the power within himself to change his destiny and to overcome evil. This movie resonated with me because I was deeply interested in transformation and personal growth. I have been an avid student of Carl Jung and Joseph Campbell, who both wrote about archetypes and myth. George Lucas, the creator of the film *Star Wars*, was also a fan of Joseph Campbell. He used Campbell's story of the hero's journey to create his characters and provide an entertaining movie that really captured people's attention. Campbell felt we all lived out this hero's journey as we sought to slay our inner dragons in our own lives. Archetypes can be the lens to better understand your own battles as well as the potential available to you.

I entered graduate school in pursuit of advanced degrees in psychology because I wanted to understand behavior—why we do what we do. Have you ever been caught up in a vicious cycle where you make choices that end up sabotaging your best intention? How do you break that cycle of sabotage and make that lifestyle change? I had been a nurse in critical care for over ten years. My colleagues and I worked and played so hard, we were basically abusing ourselves. I had worked with patients who were dying and still engaged in self-destructive behaviors. I was on a quest to understand *why*.

Why did nurses and healthcare workers not take better care of themselves when they knew better than anyone? Why did so many people settle for so little in life? Why did so many people feel so powerless to change their behavior? The light bulbs flashed for me when I met the archetypes. They told a story about the patterns we can get stuck in and when you got to know them; they offered a way out.

Archetypes are metaphors, universal patterns of behavior. They represent core qualities, positive and negative, within each of us. They are compelling because they mirror what is held deeply in our own unconscious. Carolyn Myss refers to them as the "Inner-net, the high speed psychic network," that quickly highlights patterns of behavior we can instantly relate to and recognize.

I remember working with nurses who would say, "It is not a job, it is an identity." They were living out the Caregiver, the archetypal pattern they most identified with. I have a client whose dream was to become a Navy Seal, representing the modern-day Warrior, sacrificing one's own safety for the safety of the greater good. The Child archetype gives us the awe and wonder necessary for living an inspired life. Too often, it is the Orphan that shows up with a cynical attitude, shut down to possibility and refusing to get beyond wounds. From the time we are born, we live out these universal patterns, until something wakes us up to become more authentic.

Archetypes are frequently portrayed in movies like *Star Wars* with a hero figure like Luke Skywalker because, as moviegoers, we connect on a deep emotional level, resonating with that character based on our own hidden emotions. Archetypes bring to life core characteristics from the human experience, and they tell the story of the light side and the dark side of the potential available to us all.

Very often in movies, the storyline is the hero's journey. We can all relate to this as we think about our own challenges. Joseph Campbell was well known for his book, *Hero's Journey: The Story of a Thousand Faces*, using this journey as a metaphor to highlight the spiritual aspect of life's challenges—to transform one from the two-dimensional character of the archetype to the multi-dimensional and authentic human being who has fought battles, persisted in the face of defeat, and won. The prodigal son is another story about the hero's journey. Upon returning home, he is richly rewarded. Facing life's challenges is a necessary part of self-acceptance and self-worth.

We have the choice to slay our inner dragons or to be defeated by them.

These archetypes shed light on the struggles that often stay in the shadows. As you read the following stories, think about where you are. Are you stuck in a self-defeating cycle? What do you need to learn, accept, or let go of to move forward in your life? Do you want to lighten up and learn to play? Bring out the *child* in you and express the lighter side of you? Do you need to break out of the status quo, embrace the *Rebel*, and go against the norm for greater innovation?

You can write your own movie script and cast the characters you need to be the hero in your own life. Archetypes and instincts live in the collective unconscious, that pool of unconscious resources we all share as human beings. Just about everyone can relate to and knows the characteristics of the Caregiver, Orphan, Child, Warrior, Rebel and Hero. And there are many more archetypes; I am only covering these six in this book.

We are pushed along the hero's path by facing life's challenges, giving us the opportunities to become more of who we are. Resilience is the inner drive that fuels this journey. We get to choose the character we play—the victim, the martyr, or the victor. The characters in movies that we are drawn to or repelled by represent the same "characters" that live within us, underneath conscious awareness, waiting to be discovered. As you bring this emotional energy to light, you slay your inner demons and light up the shadow element that is keeping you stuck. You also come face-to-face with your strengths that you may not have accepted until now. Here is where you find your authentic self, your inner genius. And your emotions are your guides to this deeper relationship.

Archetypes offer great insight into behavior; this is their gift when you learn their lesson and integrate its message. Each archetype represents just one piece of the whole self. It is important to learn from and discover the lesson from each. In this book, I will reveal six archetypes and also share the shadow archetypes, the Superhero and the Imposter, which steal your thunder and keep you playing small.

I weave stories of individuals stuck in each archetype. You may see yourself as you read through the book. Throughout, there will be questions so you can reflect and connect on a deeper level. Take the time to write out responses. As you explore the internal conflicts brought to light by these archetypes, you can heal the past.

Once you shed light on the patterns, it is amazing how self-defeating behavior slips away. Light destroys the shadow. With reflection, you have the chance to gather up parts of you that were discarded, because you did not then recognize their value.

If you remember in *Star Wars*, Luke had to confront his father, a Jedi Master who had gone to the Dark Side. Once Luke confronted him, he was able to easily access his innate superpower (the Force) and free himself and the entire ship from destruction.

This is the metaphor for going through a dark night of the soul and uncovering these discarded parts; once you do, you open yourself up to great potential and prosperity. This has been the purpose of myths and storytelling since the beginning of time. What stories played out in your family? Was there a damsel in distress, a revolution to fight, someone to rescue, or a Knight in shining armor waiting in the wings? Take a look at the themes that may be active in your own life. The archetypes are here to inform us. Think about archetypes as metaphors that play out at work, home, in relationships, politics, and just about anywhere a group of people gather.

I saw the Superhero being played out in everyday struggles my clients brought to me when they tried to be all things to all people. I understood the drama played out in workplaces with the shadows of these archetypes. The Orphan becomes the bully, the Caregiver becomes the rescuer, and the Child, the victim. In my doctoral dissertation, I first explored the power of these archetypes when researching the impact of change on nurses and physicians. I found the ideal Caregiver needed to integrate the lessons of the Child, Orphan, and Warrior to be self-sustaining and not burn out.

To live a fully developed life and work smarter, we all have to transform old, outdated beliefs and accept the truth of one's identity as an unlimited soul. I bumbled and fumbled my way through the challenges that showed up in my life only to have my purpose revealed to me once I accepted myself – just as a I was.

Shortly after I entered my graduate program, I had been laid off from a position I loved. I was the Clinical Specialist in a medium-sized hospital and had just created and successfully launched a program for Compulsive Eating. It was financially successful, and there was a waiting list. This was the early 90s, and hospitals at that time were going through major restructuring due to insurance reimbursement changes that dramatically cut revenue. Hospitals all over town were laying off nurses like myself who had advanced degrees. It didn't matter that my program was successful; I was now on my own.

This was the beginning of my journey as I faced paying rent, tuition, and meeting my needs *without a job*. I had just started my doctoral program and was unable to find a job as a nurse, and I was denied unemployment *because* I was a nurse. This contradiction was my first lesson in transformation; when faced with a situation that was contradictory, it is time to let go of beliefs that are blocking progress. I always believed *nursing would give me security,* and life was showing me that security did not come from my job.

*Are you living with contradictions? What beliefs do you need to let go?*

Forced to come up with a way to generate income since hospitals all over were not hiring, I launched my first consulting business. Prior, I held positions in Performance Improvement and knew I had my strengths in this area. This led me to offer services that related to quality, process improvement, and regulatory adherence. After knocking on doors for two weeks, just when my severance ran out, I had my first contract as a consultant. The timing of this was lost on me in the moment. Later, I would realize that I was creating my own experiences as I developed clarity and focus. After that, it got easier, and word-of-mouth brought me additional work. In the meantime, I was fascinated and completely absorbed in my graduate studies and wanted to learn more from my new friends—the archetypes.

Until I lost my job as a nurse, I did not realize how much I over-identified with my title and role. When I was laid off from my job as Clinical Specialist, I was more concerned with the loss of this identity than about how I would feed myself. Now that I was living outside of my comfort zone, without a paycheck and without a job, I learned so much about what I was capable of and what I still needed to learn.

Unless we embrace the potential that lives within us, we are at the mercy of the shadow side that wants to limit what is possible in our lives. Self-awareness is the light that destroys the fears of uncertainty and self doubt. Unexpected life events force awareness as we have to learn what we are capable of, in order to move forward. Do nothing and stay stuck.

## THERE IS GOLD IN THE SHADOW

*"When you are in the dark, light a candle
and bring in the light."*

The shadow contains the parts of self that you have decided are not acceptable for the light of day. From the time you were born, there have been messages that tell you to rein it in, don't show off, laugh too much, act so smart, look so good, talk loud, run fast – you name it.

How have you turned down the light on your brilliance, rounded the edges so you could fit in? For the love of your parents or your desire to maintain status quo and not rock the boat, you shaved off parts of yourself to please someone else. These parts have been tucked away because, somewhere along the line, someone told you or made you feel like it was wrong to share them with the world. By the time one reaches adulthood, most people are only conscious of a sliver of their true nature, gifts, and talents. The rest of your brilliance is hiding in the shadow.

Debbie Ford, author of *The Secret of the Shadow*, and Carl Jung both talked about one's brilliance being hidden within your shadow. This is the part of us that is ignored and maybe even hated. It is where a lot of emotions get stuck and stored away, making it a very scary place to visit. The shadow is what keeps people playing small. I have seen so many people, including myself, do this in order to belong and feel like they fit in.

Each of the archetypes has a shadow element. Most people are afraid to look more deeply at what might live in their shadows; this is where emotions are banished. And when emotions are ignored and hidden away, they may be out of mind, but they carry an intense charge that can be frightening to re-experience. Emotions are stored at the age they were experienced. When they come up again, one can be transported back to that time period, feeling vulnerable and scared.

This is why I wrote this book. Learning to identify and navigate the world of your emotions will set you free in a way that will transform your life. People in general tend to fear what they don't know. Let's elevate emotional awareness beyond that black box metaphor of the airplane. Stop waiting for a crash to learn more about them.

Fear causes you to suppress anything that doesn't fit with the "self" image you want to display. If you are a Caregiver, then taking time for yourself is completely selfish and will dismantle your identity. And this can trigger the unhealthy experience of shame. I cover shame later in the chapter on emotions.

We will see in the Orphan archetype that belonging is more important than personal growth. Most recently, I met a woman who has stayed in her job for over ten years for fear of change and starting over. Her need to feel like she belonged overrode her other need to grow personally and professionally. She said she was committed to her employer even though she was unhappy with the salary and her actual work. She was going to "stick it out." Being a martyr is typical in the Orphan archetype.

You will see in the Warrior archetype that setting boundaries is the main job of this character. In the shadow of the Warrior is the desire to fight for personal gain, raw anger, and aggression. You can get addicted to anger and probably know people whose default mode of expression is to get angry. This false confidence that comes when one rises up in anger is a poor substitute for self-worth.

Darth Vader represents the shadow warrior. Once a noble Jedi Master with great power, he had to hide behind the black Vader mask when he went to the Dark Side. Underneath, he was weak and shriveled. Your Warrior energy is needed to defend your goals and dreams. The Warrior energy sets boundaries, without apologizing and protects your dream from those who want to squelch it. The Warrior picks his battles carefully and matures with the compassion and life-giving properties of the Caregiver. Without it, the fight is simply a fight.

Are you sitting on raw aggression, afraid to let your Warrior defend your right to say no? Do you put up a fight when it is not necessary to do so? Your Warrior may be asleep in your shadow; it is necessary to confront your ability to stand up for your dream.

The Warrior archetype is important to balance the tendency to over-give as the Caregiver. The Warrior calls you to demonstrate strength, display courage, and follow through on your goals. It gives you the energy needed to overcome adversity and fight for what is yours. In the section on anger, you will learn more about what this emotion wants to tell you.

Confronting the shadow is part of every journey. Everyone must confront those beliefs that hold them back, and this usually happens when life throws a curve: getting laid off, a health challenge, a marriage ending, or something else forces a harder look at one's beliefs and values. In order to truly give from a full cup without hurting oneself, the Caregiver must learn that caring for self is essential to sustain giving. The growing edge for the Caregiver is to embrace the message of anger, as opposed to being angry, and learn to say *no* and set boundaries. This is the positive energy of the Warrior archetype.

The Child archetype has a great capacity for denial and will ignore what is really happening in order to maintain the self-image that fits his or her fantasy. This is the classic belief system of the child: denial that the parents could be at fault. Instead, the child takes the blame for everything going on in the home. This is the "baggage" you have to unload if you want to move into adulthood with a healthy sense of self. The Child has to recognize he or she is not responsible for everything that happens and cannot control things so it all turns out "just so."

Bringing your shadow side into the light of day is when you heal. As you bring your emotions out of hiding and learn to flow with their message, you will have more energy, vitality, and life in your day. How might your life open up if you were more accepting of your talents and strengths? What could it be like without the internal conflict that happens when emotions are ignored or suppressed? Learn to make friends with your emotions. Think of them as your GPS—your guide for personal success on your journey to Super Self-Empowerment.

This is a very individualized process. What would a better relationship with you look like? Would you have more fun? More love in your life? What would happen to your weight? Your health?

The wake-up call could be a health problem or change in job or relationship; either way, it forces a transition. Losing my job was that type of call. I no longer had the comfort of a paycheck every week and had to learn new ways to think of myself and how I related to the world around me.

I was thrust into a transition from employee to entrepreneur. When this happened, I remembered how much I had wanted to start a business before I went to nursing school. I did not know that was called 'entrepreneurship.' I just knew I was always interested in running a business. I was laughed at, and any effort to move in this direction was thwarted.

*What is your deepest desire? How do you honor it?*

My bachelor's degree was in Business Administration for that reason. I thought perhaps one day I would open my own business, although it was not an active thought. My mother did not think much of this idea when I was deciding what to do with my life. She made me feel as though it was frivolous and I would never succeed. She was set on my being a nurse. It was "safe and secure." And I treated my own desire the same way I was treated—I dismissed it, until I lost that security I thought was guaranteed.

In my shadow was my self-reliance, the belief that I could accomplish whatever was put before me and I could earn what I needed. In my nursing jobs, within my comfort zone, I did exercise my innovative and creative spirit and would rewrite my job description or create new programs that helped to satisfy my need to think outside of the box. Once I lost my job, it was time to actually jump off and fly. My survival depended on my ability to create my next paycheck. My mother was not going to support me. I had to pay my own way.

Up to this point, I was living with an ongoing crisis of confidence. I now had to live "as if" I was capable. The way to expedite your personal transformation is to bring awareness to parts you have ignored or pushed aside. This is accomplished by embracing the challenges that show up in your life and questioning your fears.

## THE CHILD ARCHETYPE WANTS TO BE RESCUED

*"Unless you change and become like little children,
you will never enter the kingdom of heaven."*
*—Matthew 18:3 NIV*

"Somewhere over the Rainbow" is the Child archetype's theme song. This archetype in its highest expression is positive, expects happy endings, has an enthusiastic sense of wonder, and is ready to see the good in everything. The ideal expression of the Child archetype is innocence, optimism, and being open to possibilities. This is the playful part of you that is inspired and filled with wonder at the beauty in life. The Child archetype believes in paradise. This naiveté is transformed into wisdom once the Child learns to trust itself and take responsibility for the outcomes in his or her life, releasing the need for denial.

We all start out a child and grow into adulthood—sort of, almost, maybe. Have you ever found yourself complaining that you did not get enough kudos for a job well done? Or, are you upset that there is not enough time to cut loose and act silly? You may even have had temper tantrums at work or home because things did not go your way.

If you haven't, do you know someone who does act this way? The Child archetype can show up as the under-developed child and act out like a brat or someone perpetually wounded. If someone did not receive the validation as a child to feel secure in oneself, there may be a big need for approval. Physically growing into adulthood does not automatically guarantee you develop a mature self-worth. As you continue down this HEAL path, you will find your insight and awareness is like a big pot of gold at the end of the rainbow. Having a clear and strong sense of who you are and of what you are capable will help you achieve a high degree of success personally and financially.

Remember the story of Peter Pan who never wanted to grow up and become an adult? This is an example of the shadow side of the Child archetype. In order for Peter to go on his adventures, he needed an accomplice. Peter needs to meet up with the shadow side of the Caregiver: Wendy, the rescuer.

Ilene and Chandler fit this description. Chandler was so attractive to Ilene because he was playful and adventurous. Ilene was so serious. She was taking care of her mother, and Chandler offered her playtime. What Ilene did not realize was that Chandler was caught up in the two-dimensional Child archetype and, while fun, was not capable of performing in an adult way. Holding down a job, pursuing financial security, and making a commitment were not part of his emotional repertoire.

What allowed this relationship to continue was Ilene's need to be a Caregiver and rescue Chandler from the consequences of his Childlike decisions. Ilene ended up frustrated. Chandler felt misunderstood and angry that he was being asked to grow up and take responsibility for himself. In our work together, the couple recognized they both needed to grow and actually made the healthy choice to do so outside of the relationship. Even though it was difficult to break up, Ilene realized that as she grew, she would outgrow her need to have fun at the expense of a committed relationship.

When the Child archetype is under-developed, there is an obsessive need to be playful and protected and a tendency to avoid responsibility. When things get tough, the Child wants to be rescued from it all. When this archetype takes over, there is the risk of addiction with a tendency toward denial, an irrational attitude, and a tendency to blame others. The Child is oblivious to its own inner power.

*Do you tend to be a rescuer or a nurturer?* You may be attracting the under-developed child.

We all start out innocent believing what is said, even when it is way off base. If, as a child, someone is criticized, belittled, or told he or she was selfish, awkward, and worse, the child believes it. Because to the child, the parent is always right. With a desperate need to be loved, children will blame themselves for problems in the home. This tendency to blame oneself is what keeps the Wounded Child archetype going back to abusive relationships, locked into a pattern of trying to fix the relationship. The myth they live under is that if they acted in the right way, the abuse would never happen.

Lacey loved to entertain people. She wanted to be on the stage. Her neighbor had played in "B" movies in Hollywood and offered his services to Lacey as a director. He was also an alcoholic and stumbling drunk by 12:00 noon. Instead of giving Lacey constructive feedback, he would make fun of her amateur efforts at acting. Lacey would leave their sessions in tears. This back and forth abusive relationship continued as Lacey would tell herself that it must have been something she'd done to fire up Dan's criticism.

The lesson in this archetype is that while one experiences disappointments and betrayal in life, it is not necessary to give up the possibility of happiness. The Child has to learn to take responsibility for its own life, and it can reclaim innocence and wonder in the world by letting go of illusions and denial. The gift of the Child archetype is the ability to be naïve and wise by conquering paradox.

## What the Child Archetype Offers

Gift: Innocence and Awe

Shadow: Denial

Lesson: Learn to see the value of paradox. Trust after betrayal, giving up in order to succeed, letting go to let in the new.

## Reflection

1. *What do you want to be when you grow up?*
2. *Do you repeat the same patterns over and over expecting them to turn out differently?*
3. *Are you waiting to be rescued?*

## Exercises: Grounding Yourself

1. Ground yourself by playing in the dirt, gardening, walking outside, or camping.
2. Take time to play, color, blow bubbles, or throw the football.
3. Visualize yourself as a child receiving all the love and affection you could ever want. Experience that and enjoy that feeling.

## Affirmation

I am a child of God, loved and protected.

## THE ORPHAN ARCHETYPE PLAYS IT SAFE

*"Everyone is discouraged, waiting for the other shoe to drop."*

Jenn loves her job. Ever since she was a little girl, she wanted to be a nurse. After nursing school, Jenn stayed at the hospital and worked on the same unit for twenty years. She sought out advanced certifications in her specialty. She paid for all of her training and made the decision to remain at the bedside rather than pursue a promotion, as she did not trust management. When the hospital went through restructuring, Jenn had been a nurse for over two decades. She was the mother of three boys. She was described by her peers as an excellent organizer, caring, and with a good sense of humor. She talked about loving the unit she worked on, "Because, just like on *Cheers*, everyone knows your name. I feel like I belong."

The sense of belonging is everything for Jenn. The sense of security and safety in the group is enough for her. Jenn is not in touch with what she needs to be fulfilled. Jenn nurtures herself with food. She is one hundred pounds overweight and talks about chocolate as her reward for all she has to go through in the course of the day. She blames the administration for "letting nursing down" and insists on remaining in the same position because, to her, it is safe and familiar. Stepping outside of this comfort zone and seeking a promotion or a new organization would risk losing this familiarity. She would have to confront her own feelings and her self-sabotage behavior. She is not ready or willing to step into her journey to become a more fulfilled and complete person. For now, anyway, Jenn is comfortable in the status quo.

*Are you settling for status quo?*

At the highest level of expression, the Orphan archetype is practical, empathetic, and down to earth. It needs to feel safe and be a part of the group. The myth lived out by the Orphan is that it can never feel safe. Because of the experience of abandonment, the Orphan wants to belong and fears it will never feel safe and secure. There is a tendency to play the victim and use the difficult experiences as an excuse to stay stuck. Orphans can become cynical, negative, and blame everyone else for their problems. With the strong desire to belong, Orphans often lose their individual identities to blend in with the group, putting up with abuse and bullying rather than going it alone.

One story that fully captures this archetype is that of "Little Match Girl." This short story by Hans Christian Anderson was first published in 1845. It tells the story of a young girl sent out by her father to sell matchsticks. Unable to sell any and afraid she would be beaten by her father, she sits down in an alley and lights one match after another, captivated by the vision of her grandmother in the flames. Her grandmother was the only person to love her. She froze to death caught up in this illusion. The Orphan archetype can get stuck in the need to belong, even if it is an unhealthy relationship. The Match Girl had the ability to light a fire for herself and start her own life, but that would mean acknowledging her pain of loss and moving forward anyway, taking responsibility for her life as an adult.

For Orphans to transform into more fulfilled and complete individuals, they need to realize it is okay to stand out, accept help, and take charge of their own destinies. The mature Orphan has an open heart (opposite of cynical), can be vulnerable, and recognizes we have all been wounded at some point. For the Orphan to receive the gift of transformation, it is necessary to acknowledge the wound and reclaim the lost parts of self.

The Orphan transforms itself when it recognizes there is no longer a need to abandon parts of them just because someone did it to them. Embracing the gift of the Warrior (the ability to set boundaries) and the Caregiver (the ability to feel compassion for self), Orphans can transform their need to stay stuck and move beyond their fears. Orphans have to confront their fear of standing out and embrace the ability to feel vulnerable. Orphans' transformations consist of opening up to their wounds so they can heal.

## What the Orphan Archetype Offers

Gift: Empathy

Shadow: Powerlessness, Victim, Cynicism

Lesson: To be vulnerable enough to heal from their abandonment. Recognition of how one has abandoned parts of self.

## Reflection

1. *Do you get cynical? When?*
2. *Do you feel stuck and blame your circumstances for not being able to change?*

## Exercise: Let Go and Release

Journal about any sadness you may have from relationships that disappointed you. Release the sadness and let go of those relationships.

## Affirmation

It is safe to let go of the past.

## THE REBEL WITHOUT A CAUSE

*"I like to shake things up just to get a reaction."*

The Outlaw, Free Spirit, Outsider, Troublemaker, and Wild Man are all names for the Rebel archetype. In American history, the Wild, Wild West was the home for the Rebel. The reality series, Mountain Men depict the mature Rebel, living life on their terms. We all know people who dance to the beat of their own drum and are called a "free spirit." You may be one of them. At some point, we all need to embrace the Rebel in us to uniquely express the gifts inside of us.

The Orphan can morph into a Rebel. Feeling abandoned, Orphans may feel like they will never belong and decide to rebel against authority. The shadow side of the Rebel feels powerless, expresses anger over their mistreatment, and can cross into anti-social or criminal behavior. Their personal anger is the roadblock to them learning to let go of the past. Their powerlessness keeps them from feeling like they can do anything about their situation. This can often lead to self-destructive behavior and drug use.

At the highest level, the Rebel is innovative, a free thinker, and revolutionary. They confront the status quo and challenge everyone to think outside the box. They are happy when they are helping change the world for the better. Robin Hood is an example of a Rebel, wanting to solve social problems in a revolutionary way.

It is a precarious balance to revolutionize the world and not be reckless, careless, and stubborn. Keri was determined to stop the mandatory overtime and help rescue the other nurses at her job. She worked as a cardiac nurse in a local hospital and decided she would join the Union after being forced to work mandatory overtime—again. She was so angry and felt powerless with her manager because nothing ever changed. She never brought it up to her manager and instead complained to her peers. Joining the Union made sense to her, even though she risked losing her job. The hospital did not want to have Union infiltration and did not like it when nurses took up the Union cause.

Keri was in the throes of the rebel archetype, and while her heart was in the right place in trying to protect her fellow nurses, she was blinded by her anger and stubbornness. The gift of the Rebel archetype is to learn acceptance, and with this comes humility. Many of the nurses simply accepted the situation, even though they did not like it, and decided to ride it out. They did voice their feelings; however, they were not blinded by their anger and instead focused on a solution. They talked among themselves about forming a staffing pool and set up an on-call system so they could have more control over their schedules yet still be able to cover the staffing needs on their unit.

Just like all the archetypes, in order to grow beyond the shadow, the Rebel has to learn to use their indignation and desire to serve the greater good and find innovative solutions rather than rebelling for the sake of change. Keri was intimidated by her manager's authority and refused to open the conversation to come up with ways to be fair to the staff without mandatory overtime.

## What the Rebel Archetype Offers

Gift: Acceptance and Humility

Shadow: Anger, Powerlessness, Addiction

Lesson: To learn to let go of what no longer serves you and to accept things the way they are.

## Reflection

1. *Do you fight the status quo? How so?*
2. *Does your anger blind you to better solutions?*

## Exercise: Be Present in the Moment

Practice mindfulness and stay in the moment. By learning to live in the now without using something to dull your feelings, you have the opportunity to engage the Superpower of Love. This will transform the anger, powerlessness, and grief that keeps the rebel acting within the shadow.

## Affirmation

I choose to release the negative feelings that get in the way of feeling happy.

# THE WARRIOR ARCHETYPE PROTECTS THE TERRITORY

*"The real battles are with the enemies within: fear, self-doubt, despair, and hopelessness."*

Casey always seemed ready to debate. Not realizing that his style was confrontational, he was surprised when people walked away from him or rejected his offer to get together. Casey's father was a very successful lawyer and taught Casey that in order to win, he had to fight his way to the top. When Casey lost the promotion and his wife asked for a divorce, he decided to look at himself. Casey was filled with self-doubt, even though he came across confident and self-assured. He shared with me that he felt confident when he caught people off-guard with his abrupt style of challenging people.

The expression of the Warrior archetype, as with all the archetypes, ranges from an immature expression to one that is fully developed. It is important to learn from the archetype and not overly identify with it.

The main role of the Warrior is to protect, secure boundaries, and follow through. A great story that highlights the highest expression of the Warrior is King Arthur and the Knights of the Round Table. The role of the Knights was to protect the King and his territory. They left the comfort of the castle and risked their lives to protect the inner most sanctity of the Fort and the King. When you cannot protect yourself, you may feel like a victim or hostage to people and situations. The Warrior energy is what keeps you balanced and your dreams and vision safe.

*Is your Warrior instinct out in front or hidden in your shadow?*

Casey was operating from an immature Warrior and had not learned to integrate the other archetypes for a more effective and loving way to relate to others. The shadow side of the Warrior may show up as an obsessive need for power and control. An immature Warrior views differences that are encountered with someone as a personal threat and that the end justifies the means. It is important to confront the shadow of the warrior (fears of being seen as weak, a closed heart) to release the gift in this archetype. The Warrior's gift is the ability to pursue his dream without apologizing for his strength.

Warrior energy is not bad. It is necessary, and it requires balance for it to be effective. In movies, the Warrior is portrayed in a shadow form as the villain or as an aggressor. Think about the various villains in the Batman series: the Penguin, Catwoman and others. In the fantasy kingdom of Camelot where King Arthur lived with the Knights of the Round Table, the Warrior was portrayed in a positive way. The Knights were committed to the noble cause of protecting the community and preserving the throne.

Engaging this Warrior energy doesn't mean you go to battle; it means you engage the qualities of focus, determination, nobility, and courage to move yourself forward. It is scary at first, especially if you have abandoned your ability to stand up for yourself to pursue your dream.

## What the Warrior Archetype Offers

Gift: Courage

Shadow: Bully

Lesson: The ability to stand up for oneself without an apology. Win. Win. Being comfortable with conflict.

## Reflection

1. Are you able to express your anger in a healthy way and establish boundaries?

## Exercises: Owning Your Power

1. Think of someone you consider to be powerful. Identify the characteristics of this power. Make a list of at least five.
2. Now, standing in front of a mirror, assume the Wonder Woman pose. Feet shoulder-width apart, hands on hips, and shoulders back. Looking in the mirror, repeat, "I am _____ _____" and repeat all the characteristics you identified in number one. Feel it, and experience the meaning of the words.

## Affirmation

I value myself. I take responsibility for my life.

# THE CAREGIVER ARCHETYPE LOVES TO BE NEEDED

*"Be patient with yourself. This is how you start caring for you."*

The Caregiver loves to take care of others, frequently sacrificing their own needs. I was so busy setting up the Compulsive Eating program and tending to my patient's needs, I missed all the clues that were springing up about the potential for layoffs and the opportunity to take care of myself. When this archetype takes over your identity, other parts of you are limited. And the only way you can feel good about yourself is by taking care of someone else, even if it makes you angry, tired, and lonely.

The Caregiver lives in a perpetual cycle of caring—or, more accurately, "over-caring"—and to avoid appearing selfish, does nothing to care for self. Caregivers are at risk of the very thing they fear—burnout —because of their resistance to leave the comfort zone of this over-caring role. Living in the shadow of the Caregiver is the ability to care for oneself with the same passion one cares for others.

The gift of this archetype is generosity and compassion. When you integrate the gifts from the other archetypes, like learning to set boundaries from the Warrior, you can be fulfilled in the caregiver role without sacrificing yourself. The power in archetypes comes when you deliberately engage them to accomplish your goals. Unaware of this underlying motive for your behavior and you are susceptible of being surprised and caught off guard by an emotional j\hijacking.

The Caregiver when fully realized is powerful. It is also the archetype of the Mother. The shadow of this energy pattern is the rescuer, "smotherer," and martyr. Caring too much for other people smothers the life force they need to grow into their fullest potential. The struggle is to be embraced in order to fulfill one's destiny.

Archetypes live out their myth in the form of urges and compulsive behavior, waiting to be discovered.

## What the Caregiver Archetype Offers

Gift: Compassion, Life Giving

Shadow: Martyr

Lesson: Recognition that caring for others comes from being able to care for self first. The ability to give begins with the ability to receive.

## Reflection

1. Do you feel compelled to take care of others?
2. What keeps you from taking care of yourself?

## Exercise: Learning to Receive

Journal about the things you would like to do in your life if you had more time and energy. Now, list those things you need to stop doing, or say no to, so, you have the time and energy for those things you want to do.

## Affirmation

Taking care of myself feels good. I value my ability to care for others and I choose to take care of myself first.

As you acknowledge the archetypes in your life, you make their unique meanings conscious, giving you the power to change. As the hero in your own life, will you love yourself and have compassion for the struggles you endured and celebrate the victories you have won?

If not now, when?

This transforms *you,* expanding your joys in life well beyond the roles you fulfill.

**TIP: ONE-MINUTE MINDFULNESS EXERCISE**

Sit in a chair with your feet firmly on the floor. When you are ready to go, set a timer on your phone for one minute (increase to two and three minutes as you progress). Push your feet down on the floor and stretch out your toes. Feel the floor underneath.

Bring all of your attention to your breathing. Take a deep cleansing breath; breathe in on a count of four, hold it for a count of four, and then exhale on a count of four. Repeat. Now, breathe normally and bring your complete attention to your breath. Focus on your breath as you inhale and then exhale. Let your thoughts drift. Acknowledge them, and then let them go, just like clouds drifting in the sky.

Now, bring your attention to the here and now. Just notice what you are experiencing. When a thought comes up, let it go and come back to the moment. Sitting in your chair, what do you notice? Let your mind slow way down, and every time you want to go to the incoming thought, come back to the present. Breathe.

This simple practice of mindfulness increases your self-awareness.

# CHAPTER 2

# THE SUPERHERO AND THE IMPOSTER SYNDROME

Who doesn't like the superheroes? Batman, The Hulk, Superman, Spiderman, Wonder Woman? Superheroes save the day, everyone loves them, but, in the end, they are alone, without a life of their own. This is what happens to busy overachievers who also try to save the day by taking on huge challenges. It can show up as agreeing to take on extra work without giving up anything else, saving your teenager by doing his science project, or agreeing to help out your partner at the thrift store even though it is your night to catch up. Or, your mother, brother, neighbor—you name it. Superheroes take on tremendous loads and expect they can carry them while managing the rest of their lives as well.

Does this remind you of anyone?

The Superhero sets out to make a difference, save the day, and solve all the problems—all before noon, so everyone can get to lunch. Superheroes are more than determined, ambitious, driven, focused, and committed—they also have a dark side. The dark side of the Superhero shows up with a tendency to be smug, have a judgmental attitude that others are just not as capable, and an obsessive need to win. Maybe they pick battles just to prove they can leap tall buildings and win every argument.

The shadow side to being a Superhero is also being a martyr and victim. To transform the superhero status, you have to slay the mental dragons: feeling vulnerable, feeling weak, feeling incompetent, and having low self-worth.

Sarah was one of my friends in graduate school. She was always offering to help others study and finish papers. She even baked and cooked and brought food to class. She was determined to save the day and be the hero everyone wanted. What she didn't see was that she began to alienate people because of her attitude that she was better than everyone. Before long, no one wanted to have her in the study group or share her food. Instead of focusing on her own work, she took on the role of rescuer. When she felt snubbed, instead of stepping back and reflecting on what was happening, she became angry and dropped out of school. The shadow side of the superhero reared its ugly head, and she became a martyr instead.

*What battles are you fighting inside that have you locked into the Superhero Syndrome?*

Self-worth is your ability to value your strengths, talents, and gifts. It is learned. By the time you are in first grade, you have internalized beliefs about yourself based on how other people have treated you. If you were loved, appreciated, and made to feel valuable, you also then treated yourself that way and came to believe, *I am capable.* If you were discounted, rejected, or worse, you came to believe you were not worthy or valuable and had questionable, if any, talents. One might grow up believing, *I am not capable*. This perpetuates the continual need to prove that feeling wrong.

The early beliefs that make up self-worth are based on someone else's ability to demonstrate love and support. If they are never challenged, they drive behavior for the rest of your life. Remember, we treat ourselves the *way we were treated*—at least, until we wake up.

I remember working with a president of a university in my coaching practice. He came to me because of some anxiety that was interfering with his ability to project a confident image. He had heard that my approach worked quickly, and he wanted to be over his anxiety yesterday. He also had a teenager who was getting in trouble, and they were arguing constantly. Using Tapping, we were able to quickly eliminate this anxiety. This is a tool that uses the body's energy system and quickly releases the blocked energy and restores balance. In the process of releasing the fears and the tension, he remembered being criticized early on, never feeling like he pleased his father. His father wanted him to play sports. He was a bookworm and loved to read. He wanted to be a political science major and teach. His father wanted him to play football and follow him in the family retail business.

My client's son was showing an interest in acting, the theater, and fine arts. It did not look like he would be studying the hard sciences, which was his father's choice for him. My client was still under the influence of his father's belief system, and since he never really learned to value himself, he did not know how to value his son. He was putting this same pressure on his son to be someone he wasn't. He was able to confront his shadow, his father's disapproval, and own his own incredible talents and gifts as an intellectual, which allowed him to appreciate his son's interest in the Arts.

Self-worth is a reflection of how much you value yourself. You can tell about your self-worth when you look at your beliefs and behavior. Do you feel like you deserve to have a life you love? A job that is fulfilling? A partner who loves you? Or, are you hiding behind a string of reasons why this is not possible?

Unfortunately, achievements and accomplishments in one's adult life do not upgrade those early beliefs. Those early beliefs are the foundation of your self-image—until they are challenged. The superhero's effort to be all that and more are born out of these early beliefs that compel individuals to try harder, to leap tall buildings, and set up incredible scenarios to prove these early, outdated, and false beliefs wrong. It takes a huge amount of energy to fight against these beliefs and to keep proving oneself. Trying so hard ultimately gets in the way of actually believing in oneself because exhaustion, fatigue, and failure become part of the self-fulfilling prophecy.

While some may take on the superhero role, there are also those who overachieve and never internalize their success; they go around feeling like a fraud. This Imposter Syndrome also comes from those early beliefs and keeps one locked into a cycle of self-sabotage. Imposters are usually overachievers who, despite their accomplishments, never feel like they have achieved success. Maya Angelou is in this club, indicating that even after writing eleven books, she feared someone would find her out as a fake.

The Imposter Syndrome was first talked about in 1978 by researchers Clance and Imes. They identified women who were not able to attribute their success to their own gifts or talents; instead, they felt they were successful because they worked harder than anyone, had a lot of luck, or were able to charm their way into the position. They discovered two out of five people actually feel like frauds, and 70% have felt like an imposter at some point in time.

The Imposter is susceptible to procrastination, never finishing projects and experiencing increased anxiety with the worry that someone will see through them. This causes self-sabotage and undermines future success.

Superhero or Imposter, this shadow side of the self is the result of old, outdated beliefs that continue to run scripts, driving behavior and challenging the current reality of achievement.

*Do your beliefs, feelings, and thoughts reflect the truth about you today? Or, are you stuck in the past, believing you are not capable?*

Self-worth comes from self-acceptance, self-love and self-awareness. It is a deep sense of feeling worthy and reflects how you value yourself. Self-worth is when you recognize you have value as a human being and not just because of what you can do. That is the trap of the Superhero. Self-worth is reflected in beliefs and actions you take to have the life you feel you deserve.

I remember referring to myself as an author in a conversation with a good friend, and his response was, "You are not an author. Don't you have to be on New York Times bestseller list?" Self-worth is your recognition that you have value because you say you do—it is not because of any other reason or because someone else gives you *their* permission! Yes, it is tough to feel this when you were not told this as a child or if you suffered from abuse or criticism. I am asking you to give yourself permission, *now*, to recognize you are part of the human family and a child of God, and this gives you a very special honor called grace. Now is the time to claim your self-worth.

*Are you going after a life you would love or just settling for a life because of doubt?*

Self-esteem, while important, is based on superficial criteria, and it can change quickly. Get a negative comment, and your esteem can be crushed; get a compliment, and your esteem goes up. Building your self-esteem is more about something you are going to do: lose weight, eat healthy, run a marathon, or do something else that will help you feel good about yourself. Yes, it is important to feel good about oneself. The trap here is that until you really value yourself—just because you are you—you will go the way of the Superhero and become a compulsive doer.

It is important to work on both. When you build a strong foundation in emotional intelligence, you will establish an accurate sense of *you*. You take inventory of yourself and include your strengths, your limits, and your ability to appreciate, understand, and respect yourself. It helps you live in the present rather than the past amongst old, outdated, and limiting beliefs.

*Are you ready to operate from your core, owning your gifts and talents, rather than constantly being in need of someone's approval?*

It is time to trade in your superhero cape and your fears of being found a fraud for Super Self-Empowerment, as you embrace all of you, from your very deepest desires to your daily choices.

### REFLECTION: GIVE EXAMPLES OF HOW EACH QUESTION SHOWS UP FOR YOU

1. *Is your self-worth dependent on how well you save the day?*

2. *Do you yearn to hear accolades about how wonderful you are and how much you do for everyone?*

3. *Do you rush in whenever there is a problem?*

4. *Do you feel like you are the only capable one to take on the problem?*

5. *Do you feel like no one does it as good as you?*

## TIP: SUCCESS JOURNAL

Designate a separate notebook as your "Success Journal." In this journal, list everything you have done that was successful. This means things like losing five pounds (never mind if you gained it back), baking bread, closing a million-dollar sale, getting a promotion, or walking ten minutes a day. Track *all* success.

This journal is simply a list—no editing or explaining. Just list all your successes.

Here are five reasons why this is a good idea:

1. Give yourself credit when you do well. This helps you maintain the bigger perspective when you get stuck on things you do not do so well or when your day feels like nothing has gone well and it is all your fault.
2. You start and end your day on a positive note. Read or write in your Success Journal right before you go to sleep (or when you wake up). It will help reframe your mindset.
3. This simple act of recording what you do well has a cumulative effect over time and increases confidence.
4. This takes the emotional overtones and fear out of the success experience. Reading and writing the success keeps it real.
5. Keeping this journal can become a ritual for you. Rituals are great ways to build new habits. And thought habits are super important. Writing and reviewing this journal will change how you think about yourself as you take in the "evidence" of your competence.

# CHAPTER 3

# WHY IS EMOTIONAL INTELLIGENCE SO IMPORTANT?

*"We can't solve problems by using the same kind of thinking we used when we created them."*
—Albert Einstein

Emotions are contagious, and one person's mood can influence a group of people in a good or a bad way. Do you want to have less stress? Manage your emotions and model this for others. You will find that your ability to *be* calm is going to calm everyone around you. Whether you own a business, manage other people, or are part of a team, emotional intelligence (EI) at work is going to serve you and your organization. This is also true for personal relationships. So often, the complaint in intimate relationships is that the other person does not listen or "get" their partner. EI is the way to become an ideal partner.

Emotional Intelligence (EI) is more than a trend and offers an opportunity to bring about success, joy, and satisfying relationships. It is more important than your cognitive intelligence (IQ) and is one of the strongest predictors of success. One of the most important traits of a successful person is to know oneself; this is the foundation of emotional intelligence. Self-awareness increases your awareness and understanding of others. When you know what you are feeling and recognize your impact on others, you are able to make choices that will advance the best outcomes possible.

Michelle worked in an insurance agency and always told you what was on her mind in an abrupt and direct way. She felt it was her responsibility to be "true to herself." By doing this she alienated coworkers and was passed over for any promotion. Finally, when her husband left her, she sought help. Michelle came to the office angry, indignant, and blaming everyone else for her problems. When asked if she understood emotional intelligence, she quickly said, "Of course! Mine is very strong; I will tell anybody what I think of them. I do not care." With that, she folded her arms and looked up. Defensive? Guarded? As her Coach, it was my job to go underneath the defenses that kept her locked into this spiral of defeat and help her understand her impact on others. As much as Michelle wanted to connect with other people (she shared her feelings of loneliness and isolation with me), the tone of her voice, the edge in her comments, and her defensive gestures turned everyone away.

Emotional intelligence helps you get what you ultimately want. After decades of research, the concept of emotional intelligence has matured. Roots of EI go back to the intelligence testing movement in the early 1900s when E. L. Thorndike, professor of educational psychology at Columbia University Teachers College, first identified social intelligence. From 1920 through the 1930s, attempts to measure the "ability to deal with people" essentially failed. For the next 50 years, behaviorists dominated the field of psychology and the focus was on measuring IQ. In 1983, Howard Gardner, best known for his theory of multiple intelligences outlined in *Frames of Mind: The Theory of Multiple Intelligences*, was a major influence in resurrecting emotional intelligence. He included two types of personal intelligence in his theory: interpersonal and intrapersonal intelligences.

In the 1990s, Peter Salovey and John Mayer, colleagues at Yale at the time, published the influential and important article, "Emotional Intelligence." Their model distinguished emotional intelligence from social ability and emphasized the development of emotional skills to facilitate thinking. In 1995, Daniel Goleman wrote the book *Emotional Intelligence* and introduced emotional intelligence in the context of performance. Goleman was a science journalist and spread the word of the EI concept, adapting it to predict personal effectiveness. Since then, he has gone on to adapt his EI theory of performance to the workplace and beyond. He has written many more books on the subject.

With ongoing research, EI has passed several validation milestones and meets the criteria for an intelligence fitting within Gardner's personal intelligence. Instruments measuring aspects of EI are now on the market. Much has been accomplished in the past two decades to further EI as a predictor of performance, establishing the characteristics of outstanding performers.

My definition of emotional intelligence is your ability to identify and leverage your emotions for a successful outcome. It lies at the heart of resilience—your ability to come back from a challenge. Individuals who went beyond the challenges and achieved success had a different mindset and inner game than those who did not. I saw this as resilience. It is important to find a way to keep your passion alive and sustain the required effort for success in work, life and play.

Wanting to find a solution to the problem of exhaustion, burnout and disillusionment in healthcare, I developed the Resilient Leader System, grounded in emotional intelligence. In the process of promoting this, I recognized a need to start with personal growth and introduce the emotions themselves. This is the program HEAL. It is time to bring emotions out of the shadows and increase comfort level and personal experience with emotional awareness. To succeed in most endeavors, one needs technical skills along with critical thinking, the ability to analyze data and reason, and the ability to manage and handle conflict. Emotions that are ignored or misread create conflict that sabotages performance.

Emotional distress ranks as the number one stressor at work. Conflicts with coworkers, bosses, and demanding customers cause distress, erodes self-confidence and contributes to turnover. And turnover is not good for business or for living an abundant life. When emotional conflict causes you to leave a job before you are ready, you lose momentum toward your goals and are left patching pieces together because of loss of income, security and familiarity of a job. Instead of working toward something, you have to provide basic survival needs.

Emotional intelligence is paramount to performance because of the nature of the stress reaction. Today, in the Age of Distraction, over activation of the stress reaction causes people to go through their days irritable, distracted, and reactive, leading to error, accidents, and low levels of performance and wellbeing. When the primitive stress reaction is engaged, your emotions get hijacked and thinking is compromised. In other words, you cannot think your way out of the "fight-or-flight" syndrome. Most people are stuck in sympathetic dominance (destructive physically and emotionally) and need to reset their stress set point to move into the parasympathetic (relaxation) mode where restoration happens.

Having a strong foundation of EI is when you master self-awareness and the impact you have on others. HEAL will help you build a strong relationship with yourself, the foundation of all other relationships.

Let's get back to Michelle. Michelle acted impulsively and was not aware of what triggered her defensive attitude. The first step to mastering EI is to increase awareness of those triggers. The simplest way to increase awareness is to practice mindfulness. I like to start with, *On a Count of Four, Breathe*, to reset your stress reaction and shift into relaxation.

Michelle was not aware that her approach with people was so abrupt. She was treated this way in her family and, to her, it was normal. Without the awareness of what was happening in her body, she was disconnected from her feelings and the thoughts that rose up from those feelings. Once she engaged in a regular practice of breathing and began to slow down the periods of overwhelm she was used to feeling, she became more mindful and could see when people winced at her remarks. She learned to observe others. Michelle values were to be "true to her," and she understood this had to also include valuing other people. She needed a role model.

I had her identify someone in her life who she respected and who responded in ways she thought was authentic and powerful, yet kind and respectful. As she watched this person, she was able to model her own reactions and eventually developed her own ability to be spontaneous. One of the biggest breakthroughs with Michelle was her ability to forgive herself for the past and to appreciate her desire to "be true to her" in this new and respectful way. She made friends with her anger, and instead of staying in the perpetual anger loop, feeling as though she had to set firm boundaries with just about everyone (rolling her eyes or telling them off), she was able to process her old anger at her family for the hurtful things said over the years. She reached a point of emotional freedom and formed a healthy relationship with her feelings. Now, she was ready to define her goals that are congruent with her heart and soul.

Another reason EI is important is that emotions can overwhelm people in their raw form. Developing your ability to learn from and use your emotions intelligently will give you access to more energy to be creative and to enjoy your life. Most people do not realize how much of their energy is siphoned off to hold back emotions or to manage the conflict that results from the lack of emotional awareness.

# REFLECTION: TAKE THE TIME AND WRITE IT OUT

1. *Do you know what you are feeling and why?*

2. *Do you manage your emotions to achieve the outcome you are looking for, or do you act impulsively and say things that fuel more conflict?*

3. *Are you aware of your impact on other people?*

4. *What do you want your life to look like?*

## TIP: ON A COUNT OF FOUR, BREATHE

Practice this for three minutes, five times a day. This builds your resilience muscle. Take a deep breath in on a count of four. Hold for a count of four, and exhale on a count of four. Do this three times.

Then, breathing normally, bring up feelings of gratitude, appreciation, love, and joy, and let that feeling surge through your being. Let any thought drift away and simply focus on this feeling. Do this for as long as you can—at least fifteen seconds.

Recall times when you were blessed, felt appreciative, or experienced love. This could be when you were struck by the beautiful colors in the sky, were in a garden, or saw flowers along the road. It could be when you witnessed a dog or cat playing and having fun or maybe a child laughing. Keep your thoughts focused on simple everyday experiences that tend to get dismissed in the course of the day when you are engaged in the "important" stuff.

Set the timer on your phone for three minutes, do the four-count breath several times, and then breathe as you hold thoughts of gratitude, appreciation, or love. If you drift, just bring yourself back to these thoughts. If you are used to racing through your day, start with one- minute and increase by one-minute increments.

Anything you do has a *cumulative* effect. Every little bit helps. Set a timer throughout the day as a reminder.

Start now.

# CHAPTER 4
# BURNED OUT TO BRILLIANT

*"In dealing with those who are undergoing great suffering, if you feel 'burnout' setting in, if you feel demoralized and exhausted, it is best, for the sake of everyone, to withdraw and restore yourself. The point is to have a long-term perspective."*
—Dalai Lama

What does it mean to be burned out? How does it show up, and who is experiencing it?

In the general population, 70% indicate they have at least one major stressor, and 25% say their job is their main stressor. Over 60% of callouts are due to stress. With information overload and the demand to multi-task—along with added stressors within the family—more people report severe stress than ever before.

The term burnout was coined in 1972 by psychologist Herbert Freudenberger, who described emotional exhaustion, alienation from the job, and lower performance as the three main symptoms of burnout. There really isn't any agreement among professionals on what burnout is or how to diagnose it.

To make this even worse, the nature of burnout obscures this devastating syndrome from the person affected, so you do not even know you have it. Burnout robs you of the awareness that there is a problem. It replaces your potential and your confidence with a cynical, hopeless belief that nothing will change. The longer someone experiences emotional exhaustion, the more feeling numb and shutdown seems like a good idea. This new normal continues to alienate the victim from positive people who can offer an alternative perspective from the negative and hopeless viewpoint.

Burnout is devastating because it robs you of the belief that things will get better and that you are in charge of your own life. Burnout doesn't happen overnight. It is the result of a prolonged and unchecked stress response. Stress is not necessarily bad; in fact, a certain amount of stress is what helps people get into the flow state. We are going to talk about flow later in the book.

## THE STRESS REACTION

The stress reaction is a primitive survival instinct. It is hardwired in the nervous system and has not changed in 200,000 years. The stress reaction is instinctive and, when triggered, takes over the rational part of the brain—the cortex. When stressed, first you feel, and then you think. Stress can make you act stupid.

Walter Canon identified the fight-or-flight syndrome in 1915. Hans Selye described the syndrome and recognized that stress can make you sick. Selye identified three stages of stress:

1. The Alarm Stage: the stressor is noted by your body.
2. The Resistance (or Adaptation) Stage: your body effectively mobilizes all resources to adapt, and your body resumes homeostasis.
3. The Exhaustion Stage: your body is depleted from the adaption process, and your body does not have the hormones, nutrients, and reserve to restore balance.

Today, researchers know that the body isn't necessarily depleted of the hormones; rather, it is the chronic nature of the stress reaction and the flood of cortisol that causes disease. If your blood pressure rises when you are fleeing danger and then returns to normal, the stress reaction has done its job. However, if your blood pressure goes up every time you step into your office, then you are at great risk for heart disease.

The body is brilliant at maintaining homeostasis and restoring the needed balance so the vital organs can function. However, it comes at a steep price. Chronic stress can compromise the immune system, leaving one open to a host of diseases, including cancer. The brain, while stimulated by one set of hormones under the stress reaction, is also damaged by another set of hormones with too much stress. The stress reaction short circuits the brains ability to make good decisions and exercise good judgment. The stomach lining thins out, and digestive trouble can occur. The list of potential health challenges as a result of chronic stress is long. In fact, some reports indicate as much as 90% of visits to the doctor are due to a stress-related symptom, and over 60% of all disease has its origins in the stress reaction.

Yes, stress can increase your risk of getting sick. However, it is not inevitable. How your body experiences the stress reaction is determined by your perception of what is happening. Most of the stress reaction today is due to imagined problems that never occur. Traffic, deadlines, trouble with your children, your spouse, your boss, money, and your friends all come with a set of thoughts, feelings, and expectations. It is what you tell yourself, what you feel, and what you believe that makes stress toxic or not.

## BRILLIANCE: BECOMING SELF-AWARE

The stress reaction in the body is primitive and based on survival. Your self-awareness is what will take you from just getting by to getting ahead. Tune into what is going on in body, mind, heart, and soul. Waking up to what is going on within you is your ticket to freedom and success.

One reason people are not successful in following through on New Year's resolutions is because they are unaware of the emotions that drive behavior. They focus on *not* doing something and rarely define what they want to have happen with the new lifestyle change.

Let's say you want to lose weight; the focus may be on *not* eating certain foods rather than becoming a person who easily makes healthy choices. When you focus on avoiding certain foods, without realizing it, you are focusing on the need for comfort food and exposing yourself to these emotional drivers that keep you making the same choices over and over. Being self-aware is the secret to changing habits and being the person you desire to be.

How do you go from autopilot to being aware? It takes practice and desire. Mindfulness is the simple act of being present and observing what is happening without the desire to change it. Try this right now: take a deep breath and exhale. Now, just bring your attention to yourself. What do you notice? Mindfulness is the deliberate focus of your attention. With chronic multi-tasking and the addiction to being busy, most people are not aware of what is happening in the moment. So much is lost without the ability to be present.

Give yourself permission to turn off your phone for periods throughout the day. Turn it off during meetings, meals, while driving, and during your quiet time. Start a new habit at home or at your job and have technology-free zones. At first, you may find yourself irritated that you cannot have access, fearing you may miss something. Stick it out because you will learn to relax more and actually have meaningful conversations with your family or coworkers. Without the constant distraction, you will be surprised at what you notice and how much more creative you can be.

In the chapter on superpowers, I share the Reboot series of exercises. This is when you reboot your attention, focus, or thoughts, bringing yourself back into the moment.

Here is the *Attention Reboot.*

Breathe on a count of four. In on four. Hold for four. Exhale on four. Repeat for three breaths. Now, take a look at the problem or situation as if it were the very first time you were seeing it. What do you notice? Your only job is to observe. Let any thoughts drift away and notice.

Now that you have reset your attention, build on your observations. Let's go back to the issue of weight loss. Someone may say they want to lose weight, but they overeat at meals and have dessert every night. Look beyond the behavior to the thoughts underneath it. Very often, this person will say, "No matter what I do, I can't lose weight." And, if you explored the feelings underneath these thoughts, you might find feelings of helplessness. Going beyond the feelings, you might also notice tension in the neck, shoulders, and increased heart rate. You can intervene at any point, behavior, thoughts, feelings, and physical experience, and when you change one reaction, you break through that block to successful weight loss.

What would help someone who feels helpless? Resources. Here is where Weight Watchers or a Coach will be ideal to provide support. Use relaxation methods to reduce tension in the body. Walk, stretch, dance, move to release that tension.

Focus on these areas and food becomes less of the problem. Food has become the substitute and distraction from these other feelings. .

Tune in to your body, your behavior, underneath your thoughts, into your feelings, and build an awareness of what is happening. As you connect at any level, you will experience insight and relief from the tension of holding everything inside.

To increase your awareness at each stage of this process, do the scan below several times a day.

## Behavior → Thoughts → Emotions/Feelings → Body

### Ask yourself these questions:

*What am I feeling?*

*Why am I feeling this?*

*Is this feeling relevant to what is happening right now, or is it based in the past?*

You can intervene at any point along the above continuum and change your choices and habits.

## Try the "body scan"

Starting at the top of your head and scanning to the bottom of your feet, check in at all levels. What do you notice?

Where are you tense, tight, wound up? Then ask what feelings show up?

Journal your observations for 90 seconds.

You are in charge and in control.

# CHAPTER 5

# RESILIENCE: PATH TO TRUE HAPPINESS

Resilience is your ability to bounce back and keep going. It is the ability to be strong and deeply connected to one's core values. Resilience is the inner game of success and shows up in a positive attitude, daily choices that support your goals, true confidence, energy to follow through, and the connection to your purpose. We are all capable of resilience, and yet, many do not activate it on a day-to-day basis.

In my private practice, more and more people wanted to learn how to thrive in their lives and not just get through the day. Resilience is the antidote to burnout and fatigue and the "force" that will keep you enjoying your life, despite the challenges that show up. For many years, I taught stress management techniques. About five years ago, I recognized I needed to help my clients *become* resilient in order to keep up with the demands of everyday life and still be creative, resourceful, and passionate. It was significant for my clients to shift from focusing on the problem and focus on the solution—becoming resilient.

Overwhelmed and being stressed out was also a symptom of the constant distraction and lack of focus that comes with increased technology taking over more of everyone's lives. I see resilience as the new way to approach work, life, and play. Becoming resilient means you are no longer victim to the stress reaction. When you manage your attention and increase your awareness, you are able to tap into the best of your talents and skills to keep going.

*What does resilience look like for you?*

*Why do some have it more than others?*

*How can you activate resilience?*

The term *resilience* in the physical sciences means to have the capacity to bend without breaking and to return to the original shape. When people go through a tough time and get through it, there is a deeper understanding or appreciation of themselves and the situation. They are transformed in the process. They have bent and may have broken, but kept going. They have greater depth and awareness in the end. Winston Churchill said it best: "If you are going through hell, keep going."

In *Resilience: The Science of Mastering Life's Greatest Challenge*, Southwick and Charney explore resilience in the context of trauma, the battlefield, and tragedy. I want to introduce you to resilience as an internal resource you can call up when you need it—every day. If you live in a chronically stressed out mode, you are going to be hijacked by your emotions and unable to think clearly and make effective decisions. This is the nature of what happens in stress with the flooding of cortisol. You lose the connection to your rational judgment. Without a way to interrupt this primitive survival instinct, burnout is inevitable.

*Do you know what experiences are the most draining for you?*

Central to resilience is the partnership with your heart's intelligence. When the stress reaction hijacks rational thought and sets up the false sense of urgency, being grounded in a sense of gratitude, purpose, and appreciation of what matters the most will help you bounce back and keep going. Being open, caring, and present—even in the face of adversity or challenge—is the antidote to burnout.

How do you stay open and present when so much is happening all around you? Resilience is this buffer, the ability to stay clear and focused in the midst of stressful circumstances. And the driver of resilience is the ability to speak the language of the heart.

## THE LANGUAGE OF THE HEART

For centuries, the heart has been considered the center of life. Early cultures, such as the Greeks and Egyptians, identified the heart as the core of an individual's emotions, decision-making, and morality. The Old French word *corage* meant *heart* and *innermost feelings*. The heart, with its symbolic meaning, has long been the focal point for understanding human existence.

In Judeo-Christian traditions, the heart represents beauty, harmony, and balance. In the Yogic tradition, the heart is the seat of individual consciousness. In the Kabbalah, the heart is the key to radiant health, joy, and wellbeing. Since ancient times, the heart was thought to have an intelligence that unified the body, mind, and spirit. Today, as energy fields are researched and technology advances, it can now be shown that the heart is much more than a pump.

Like many organs in your body, your heart has its own system of communicating with the rest of the body. The heart has the strongest energy field, extending twelve to fifteen feet from the body in all directions. The heart initiates communication with the entire body to bring about stress relief and personal transformation. Whether you connect with your heart in prayer, meditation, mindfulness, or other breathing techniques, your heart provides a deep source of wisdom, peace, and balance. In contrast, your "thinking" brain has limits and is unable to unhook you from fast-track triggers initiated during stress responses. It is actually *why* you are triggered in the first place!

Your heart communicates with the rest of the body in a way that once was thought impossible; with its network of hundreds of thousands of miles of blood vessels and 75 trillion cells, along with thousands of messenger molecules at its service, your heart is an information and energy transmitter and receiver. Your heart wants to communicate with you through your intuition, wisdom, gratitude, appreciation, and love and give you greater peace and clarity.

Most people have separated intelligence from wisdom, not believing they are related. Today, scientists, holistic practitioners, and wise mystics all recognize the heart's language and ability to "persuade" the rest of the body to de-stress. If people were not caught up in a "time and demands" gridlock, the heart's message might be more easily heard, reducing the negative impact of stress.

Many people believe it is the brain that moderates the response to stress. In an amazing research project, Paul Pearsall, PhD, author of *The Heart's Code* and researcher of the relationship between emotions, the brain, and the immune system, or *psycho-neuro-immunology*, identified that the brain tends to dominate at the expense of better, more meaningful, and more efficient interactions we might have with the world around us. Engaging the heart's intelligence enables deeper insight, wisdom, and greater clarity. Dr. Pearsall studied recipients of heart transplants and the remarkable stories they would tell about their organ donors that they would have no way of knowing except by way of their new hearts' intelligence. He went on to demonstrate that the intuition they received was part of the heart's powerful communication network.

With heart disease, the number-one killer in this country, it would seem the sooner you can accept and connect with the "dominion of the heart," the healthier and more vibrant you can be. Making this connection is also a way toward greater peace in general.

Researchers Dr. Gary E. R. Schwartz and Dr. Linda G. S. Russek also found that the body is constantly communicating with itself, capable of transforming or altering itself in the process. Their research confirmed what Pearsall found, that the heart sends "info-energy" throughout the body, influencing every cell. Their book, *The Living Energy Universe: A Fundamental Discovery that Transforms Science & Medicine*, draws attention to this neglected arena of scientific research. This field of "cardio-energetics" continues to build momentum, promoting the heart's influence in overall wellbeing. The notion of an intelligent heart is now more than an idea. After decades of research, it is now recognized that the heart communicates both energetically and through thousands of messenger molecules, relaying information throughout the body, changing thoughts and emotions and improving health.

Now that we know this communication takes place, why not engage this process deliberately and communicate from *it* rather than the limited perception present in a stress reaction? This is the nature of resilience, the intentional partnership of heart, mind, body, and soul.

When the heart is focused on core feelings such as love, appreciation, and caring, heart rhythms actually change. The Heartmath Institute has researched the heart's ability to communicate with the body and found the following changes take place when this intelligence is engaged. The communication between the heart and the rest of the body produces a biochemical effect influencing every organ and system in the body. One main effect is increased efficiency when engaged in a stress reaction. The following effects have been noted:

- Decreased production of cortisol, the stress hormone
- Indirect increase of DHEA, your anti-aging hormone
- Increased levels of the IgA immune antibody group, strengthening the immune system
- Greater clarity of thought
- Improved focus
- Lowered blood pressure

Can you see why it is so important to interrupt the stress reaction? It shuts down your connection to the wisdom coming from your heart.

*What is it your heart wants you to know?*

## FORGIVENESS: THE KEY THAT UNLOCKS THE DOOR TO YOUR HEART

I do not remember her name. She was in her early thirties and came to me for a fear of public speaking. She wanted to be hypnotized so she could comfortably speak to a crowd. She had been promoted, and her new role involved frequent impromptu speeches. When she came in, my intuition told me there was much more to this fear. The client was not aware of anything in her own life that would have caused her reaction to public speaking. After all, it is the number one fear, and it made sense to her that she would be afraid.

As we explored her history, she shared she had a life-threatening reaction to shrimp. Following my intuition, I asked more questions about where, when and what her reaction was like. She remembered a time in her teens when she was eating shrimp at a family party and her uncle walked into the room. This was the uncle who sexually abused her; no one else knew because she never told anyone. Even though she had put it out of her mind, her body remembered that incident and immediately reacted. Once we cleared the trauma and she was able to forgive her uncle, her fear of public speaking disappeared. (So did her reaction to shrimp!)

Forgiveness comes once you realize that holding on to the hurt no longer serves you. Very often, the anger and hurt shields one from feeling the pain of loss or betrayal; it also blocks you from receiving love and other good things. Forgiveness is your way to open the door to greater joy, love, and emotional freedom.

*What are you holding onto that no longer serves you?*

Forgiveness is a shift in thinking. Rather than blaming someone for what they did to you, there is a release of the blame and an acceptance of what happened. By taking ownership of what happened and its impact on you, you release the other individual and free yourself from this conflicted relationship.

To forgive means you move on. It doesn't mean you both come together and reconcile your differences, nor does it mean you forget about the incident or that you make excuses for what happened. It means you have a neutral feeling toward that person with no further need from that person.

Sometimes, holding on to the anger keeps one connected to the person, and this can happen with unmet needs. You will feel more fulfilled if you find a substitute for those needs and release the individual you are upset with along with the anger, bitterness, and grief and simply let it go - forgive.

Forgiveness is powerful. It is an act of self-love and kindness toward you. It is not something you do for anyone else. Forgiveness helps you release the tie to that person and frees you to experience the greater fulfillment in relationships. Holding that grudge or feeling victimized blocks your ability to experience joy in other relationships. Holding on to that experience blocks you from seeing what is possible day to day.

# CHAPTER 6

# YOUR BODY TALKS: ARE YOU LISTENING?

*"Healing is a matter of time, but it is sometimes also a matter of opportunity."*
—*Hippocrates*

Becky wants to stay home and not attend the family picnic. She has precious time to finish up her paper and catch up on her sleep. Her family insists she attend the picnic that has been planned since last year. Frustrated, fighting off the guilt, and trying not to let her anger show, she tells them she has to stay ahead of her schoolwork. Her family thinks the three twelve-hour shifts she works are the same as working part time.

Stewing, Becky thinks to herself, *Don't they understand how long a twelve-hour shift is? And I am in school, too. All they think about is how it will look if I am not there. All I can think about is the wasted energy on feeling so guilty, and even if I stay home, I have lost my momentum. I just cannot win sometimes.*

Being sandwiched between guilt, anger, and obligation is a dilemma for many mothers, fathers, and professionals who want to balance family and career.

Becky ends up going to the picnic, only to act out her resentment with an off-handed comment to her sister that creates tension between them. Becky usually gets along with her sister and is too overwhelmed to realize the damage to this relationship. She also goes into work tired *again* and feels bad that she is not able to give it her usual 100%. Becky knows that being a perfectionist is part of her conflict. She tries hard to please everyone and usually forgets that, ultimately, *she* needs to be happy. Feeling resentful that no one really understands and trapped in her need to be perfect, Becky starts to have indigestion and heartburn. She is too caught up in the free floating emotional storm to realize her tension and resentment is burning her up on the inside.

Becky's story is an example of how emotions can bottleneck within, compromising one's health. What if Becky could tune in and listen to what her heart wanted her to know or she learned to respect her anger and set better limits? Emotions are part of your nervous system and require expression. One way or another, they will express themselves.

Let's look at how stress and the feelings of frustration, conflict, and overwhelm distort your relationship with healthy emotions.

## STRESS AND YOUR EMOTIONS

First, "stressed out" is not an emotion, and the feelings associated with being "stressed out" are usually a combination that results from not being able to identify and name the feelings involved. The frequency of stress reactions and their intensity are clues about your relationship with your emotions. First, the actual stress reaction is a primitive reaction designed as a survival instinct. The fight-or-flight mechanism triggered by the stress reaction requires some type of action.

Today, the majority of people live in some type of hyper-vigilant "freeze mode" with an ever-present stress reaction running in the background. This may explain the flashes of rage, irritability, and sarcastic reactions that occur all too commonly.

Living in a chronically stressed-out mode blurs your ability to identify and understand feelings because of the dominant fear reaction trigged by the amygdala. The amygdala is part of the primitive brain (designed for survival and not day-to-day interactions) that hijacks your reactions, bypassing the rational and logical cortex of your thinking brain. The amygdala's purpose is to generate a reaction of fight-or-flight to guarantee survival; this hyper-alert emotional trigger is designed to be short-lived and naturally followed by a relaxation mode. Unfortunately, that is not what happens. Most people today are stuck in the middle of a hyper-alert state and do not enter that period when the nervous system relaxes and restores itself.

Awareness helps you go underneath your knee-jerk patterns of reaction and establish a relationship or conversation with your healthy emotions. This, in turn, will help you change your reaction to stressful triggers and situations. Without emotional self-awareness, just about anything has the potential to cause stress and sabotage your health.

Becky's emotions, guilt, and anger were cues that she needed to set limits with her family. Instead, she treated herself the way she was treated (dismissing her needs for the sake of getting along with her family) rather than the way she wanted to be treated and ended up in emotional turmoil with physical distress. Becky needs to relate differently to her emotions of guilt and anger around obligation and understand what these emotions want her to do, like setting boundaries with her family. This self-knowledge would enable her to effectively communicate her needs while also respecting the needs of her family.

Little did I know, I would eventually open an Integrative Health practice and help individuals partner with their emotional, physical, energetic, and spiritual selves. Today, I continue to highlight the power of emotional intelligence, especially for healthcare professionals, to enable a better quality of life for them and a better healing experience for the patient and healthcare institution.

The connection between the mind, emotions, and body is better recognized and more thoroughly studied now than when I started my Integrative practice twenty-five years ago. Today, it is accepted that the immune system is intimately tied to emotions. Emotions, when not accepted or acknowledged, cause physical harm. Becky is just one example of what unexpressed emotions can do. You don't heal by acting as though you do not have any feelings; you heal when you tune in, listen, and acknowledge what you feel and then take some action based on their message.

Can you really control the physical functions in your body? Can you use the wisdom of your emotions to improve your health? Yes, you can. Daily choices in the way of diet and lifestyle have a significant impact on your health, and even more important are your choices in how you feel, the thoughts you choose, and the attitude you have toward yourself and your life. You are more than just a body, and your emotions will either help or hurt your physical body.

Barbara Levine, author of *Your Body Believes Every Word You Say*, explored mind, body, and emotional connections. In Levine's book, she shares many studies wherein scientists have demonstrated the connection between what we feel and think and the activity of the immune system. In study after study, evidence supports the link between emotions and disease. Antonio Damasio, the neuroscientist, also writes in his book, *The Feeling of What Happens*, about emotions that are outside of conscious awareness and yet impact the cellular activity of the body.

Is it true that emotions translate into body language? In my own practice, I was always amazed by how body, mind, and emotions communicate within my clients and the connection between unexpressed feelings and physical illness. It was my job to help my clients navigate their "bodytalk." I believe that any symptom that shows up offers an opportunity for you to learn more about yourself by exploring the symptom in the context of mind, body, heart, and soul. Why not use this communication from the body as a wake-up call for more vibrant health?

*What would you do with more harmony and less conflict in your day?*

Once, a client came to see me for a chronic sinus reaction. She was tired of taking antibiotics, steroids, and nose sprays and not getting the relief she wanted. I practiced NAET (an acupressure technique to change the body's overreaction to foods, pollens, etc.). Recognizing the connection between mind, body, and spirit, I saw the opportunity for my client to heal on multiple levels, not just on the physical level of the sinus reaction. My intuition suggested I ask about her mother. The client was amazed I asked because she had been struggling with a conflicted and difficult relationship with her mother. We used Tapping and NAET to shift the body's energy related to this emotional conflict with a successful clearing of emotions *and* sinus congestion. The client walked out of the office after one session with clear sinuses and a sense of relaxation she said she had not felt in at least five years.

When she came in for her follow-up appointment, she said that after three days, the symptoms returned. I asked her what was going on during that time. First, she told me about how shocked she was that this method actually worked, and she kept saying over and over, "I just can't believe it worked." Her mother had stopped by, and they ended up in another one of their conflicts. It took a few more sessions with insight and awareness on the client's part to recognize that healing happens at many levels of mind, body, and spirit. She did clear up her sinuses using a combination of techniques to support a healthy gut, shift her emotional energy, heal conflict, and build emotional awareness. As she partnered with her emotions, she found a new confidence in her relationship with herself, allowing a better relationship with her mother.

What do your emotions want you to learn?

# CHAPTER 7

# UNDERSTANDING EMOTIONS

*"Genius is the ability to renew one's emotions in daily experience."*
—*Paul Cezanne*

"We do not think you are a good fit for our organization. We are letting you go."

Stunned, Amy left the meeting in shock. She had worked for this hospital for over twenty years. *Not a good fit? I was good enough to get them through the accreditation and work all those weekends,* thought Amy. She felt herself getting really angry and wanted to tell someone what she really thought. Instead, she gathered her things and left. Walking out of that hospital after 20 years was really hard. Her legs felt so heavy, like she was in slow motion, and she started crying as soon as she got in the car. Still in disbelief, Amy began to shut down as she told herself, *Pull yourself together. Crying is not going to change anything.*

She stopped crying and drove home. Immediately, she got on the internet looking for another job. It wasn't critical she work immediately; she did have a small severance, and her husband was working. Looking for a job made her feel better and kept her from the flood of emotions just waiting to take over.

In the days and weeks that followed being let go, Amy had trouble sleeping. She was irritable, restless, and achy. She lived on coffee and chocolate to keep going during the day. To relax at night, Amy drank wine. In hindsight, she realized she felt hopeless, old, and outdated. Amy graduated from a diploma program, and because of her dedication, her people skills, and her commitment to doing a great job, she had been promoted over the years to Manager of the Outpatient Surgery Department. She had been encouraged to go back to school to get her BSN. However, due to raising her daughter with a rocky marriage, it just did not seem like the right time. Amy enjoyed her position and loved the nurses and docs she worked with, but wasn't sure she wanted to dedicate more of herself to this type of nursing. She did not want to be on call for the rest of her life or deal with the extended days. She wanted to plan her days and have weekends off.

A few months ago, the dermatologist she went to, shared his vision for opening a MedSpa. He needed someone like Amy to manage the aesthetics services and help him grow the business. It was just what she wanted: regular hours, the chance to get to know her patients, and weekends off. She was afraid to step out of her comfort zone and go for it. She had not even realized how excited she was about the possibility, because she kept telling herself, *This will never work. I have been at my job for so long; I might as well retire there.*

Amy came to me after several more weeks of internal torture. Feeling like a failure, not sleeping, and drinking wine at night and coffee during the day, she had also gained ten pounds. Her husband wasn't speaking to her, and she still could not bring herself to think about what happened. She wanted help sleeping. I explained the tools of my trade, and we were able to use Tapping, visualization, and hypnosis to release these blocked emotions. In just three sessions, Amy was able to accept what happened. In hindsight, she also remembered some warning signs that led up to being fired; she had missed them being too busy taking care of everyone else.

In this section, we are going to explore these questions:

- What are emotions?

- Why do you have them, and what do they want from you?
- Are emotions and feelings the same?
- What are moods?
- Are emotions simply an involuntary response to what is happening in your environment?
- Are they universal social cues or merely a biochemical response in the body?
- What happens to an emotion if you are not conscious of it happening?
- Like the tree in the forest, if no one is around, does your emotion still exist?

### WHAT ARE EMOTIONS?

Scientists cannot agree on the definition of emotions. Sociologists, psychologists, neurologists and other "-ologists" all have a different idea of what emotions are. Some describe emotions as involuntary reactions to what is going on around us. Others define them as universal phenomena with each of us getting a basic set of human emotions, at birth, as "standard issue."

For the rest of us, navigating our own and others' emotions in the process of life and work, a better understanding of emotions will make the difference between success, disaster, and a standstill. We all have had the experience of an emotional hijacking when we were caught off-guard by our emotions and found ourselves acting out of character. It is important to have a way to identify, understand, and relate to our emotions.

Awareness is the foundation of emotional intelligence. Since we live in a society where emotions are considered secondary input at best (and even evil by some), identifying emotions can be difficult. Depending on the culture in your family or at work, you may not have permission to express your emotions. If you are in a culture without emotional awareness, you can be shamed for expressing your emotions.

I was in my late twenties working in a neurosurgical ICU in a university hospital. This was my tenth year working in critical care settings. A young man, about my own age, came to the emergency room having had the worst headache of his life. He ended up having an aneurysm in the main arterial blood supply to the brain. He was transferred to our unit for stabilization before we could transfer him to a specialist in another hospital who would operate on that aneurysm. I worked twelve-hour nights and around 2:00 a.m., I went into his room to change his dressings and do my assessment. The patient was sleepy but alert, and we exchanged a few smiles. As I was putting on the last piece of tape, he opened his eyes and screamed out in pain. At that moment I saw his pupils dilate. I called for the code and the emergency process started.

During the code, I focused and did my part. After the code, I sat down at the nurse's station and cried. The Chief Resident of Neurosurgery came over to me and yelled, "If this is how you act, how will you ever make it as a nurse?!" He walked out.

That was a turning point in my nursing career. Leading up to this particular instance, I had already been involved in scores of codes. I had witnessed people dying, held hands with young and old, and spent hundreds of nights working in a trauma setting. On that day, however, I wondered why I was the only one that cried? What was normal anymore?

The Chief Resident was known for his outbursts. Most of the nurses excused this behavior, because, after all, it takes a lot to focus for twelve or more hours doing microsurgery and then be on-call. I did understand that. What I did not understand at that time was that certain feelings like anger were okay to be expressed by physicians and other feelings like sadness were taboo. What was wrong with my expressing sadness? I felt shame for being so vulnerable and was confused about what was acceptable.

Families and organizations both carry mixed messages related to expressing emotions. On the one hand I was expected to be caring and sensitive and on the other, to hold everything inside. In these environments it is easy to feel like it is your fault when you are criticized for expressing yourself. Instead, tune into your feelings and take care of you.

*What do you need to restore your internal balance?*

## WHY DO YOU HAVE EMOTIONS AND WHAT DO THEY WANT FROM YOU?

Emotions are signals providing cues for us to take some type of action. Since most of us grow up with little training or role modeling in the healthy expression of emotions and work in a culture where emotions are preferably, neither seen nor heard, it can be quite the challenge to identify an emotion and figure out what it is telling you.

Antonio Damasio, Head of Neurology at the University of Iowa College of Medicine and author of the book *The Feeling of What Happens*, defines emotions as "complicated collections of . . . responses, forming a pattern . . . [with a] regulatory role to play . . . to assist the organism in maintaining life". He acknowledges that emotion and reason are related and goes on to describe emotions as "the result of a long history of evolutionary fine-tuning." In other words, we all come equipped with a collection of emotions as part of our survival kit.

In other words, emotions are hard wired and necessary for our survival. Charles Darwin found similarities in emotions across cultures, and he wrote about them in his book *The Expression of the Emotions in Man and Animals*. Emotions ensure survival. The message that "one can separate one's emotions and still function well" is a myth. We are biologically hardwired to use emotional cues to make decisions and get through our day. Survival depends on the recognition of emotional cues.

The limbic system is the place in the brain where emotions live. About the size of a walnut, the limbic system consists of the parts of the brain that are involved in emotional memory and motivation. Structures such as the amygdala, olfactory bulb, and hippocampus (to name a few) play an important role in the expression of emotions. This region of the brain, sometimes called the "feeling" brain, sits underneath the cortex, or the "thinking' brain."

Here is one time when *size doesn't matter*. The size of the cortex might imply power over the smaller structures of the brain; however, as we mentioned before, the amygdala is part of the survival instinct of the primitive brain and is capable of triggering an emotional hijacking that will throw off even the smartest intellect. The hypothalamus is also an important structure responsible for emotional reactions and many regulatory functions, like appetite. This may partially explain why food is the primary "go-to drug" for most people when responding to stress.

The fact is, first we feel, and then we think. These feelings can be exaggerated and in accurate. It pays to develop awareness and mindfulness related to your emotions in order to manage the impact your emotions will have on another.

If emotional triggers can happen at any time, short-circuiting your capability for rational thought, then how "safe" are you from such "attacks?" The more your emotional body is outside of your awareness, the more vulnerable you are to an emotional hijacking. Later, I share the Five Superpowers to help you stay in flow with your emotions.

It is a good thing that science is finally catching up with what we know intuitively: one cannot separate emotions, or turn off a significant part of ourselves, without the risk of losing another very important part. When you shut down some part of your emotional body, you shut down or warp the expression of all emotions. Joy, happiness, empathy, and love are all diminished if you shut off emotions like sadness, anger, or fear. Emotions inform and instruct. By tuning in to their wisdom, you are turning on a greater awareness and larger life force accessible for you to live a full life. When you shut down your emotions, you do so at the risk of also shutting down your life force.

Antonio Damasio, in *Self Comes to Mind*, reinforces that emotions are automatic. They are not "learned," but rather inborn "action-requiring" neurological events, meaning your emotions require you to take action. This is not acting out the emotional charge – this happens when your emotions are outside of your awareness. Emotions are natural and imbued with a message, yet, too many people are not able to name their feelings or manage them.

Healthy emotions are fluid and fleeting. When emotions get stuck, their expression is distorted as a result of stuffing them, hiding them, and doing just about anything to avoid them. Eventually, they will be expressed.

Emotions are like a child: they want to be acknowledged, or they continue to tug at you until they get your attention. When they do finally get expressed, it is usually awkward or excessive. That is what happens when you hold back and store up all that energy. We talked about how the body expresses stored up emotion in dis-ease. Emotions are a vital part of your communication within body, mind, heart and soul. I want to help you navigate better and learn the message your emotions have for you.

Emotions can be evoked as a result of real or imagined situations. You may start to feel fear when you think the tickle in your throat is much worse than just a cold coming on, and, before long, your mind has strung together "facts" that all seem to fit, leaving you with the conclusion that you are very, very sick. For this reason, it is important to understand yourself and what your typical emotional patterns are. Are you prone to fear?

If you tend to be afraid of just about everything, something is out of balance and requires an adjustment. Emotions are designed to be fleeting—not running in the background nonstop.

## EMOTIONS, MOODS, AND FEELINGS

While identifying and relating to emotions is easy for some, others are not aware they are experiencing emotions until the feelings of sadness, anger, or fear persist and become a mood.

Emotions are the name you give to the feelings you experience in your body, while moods are the persistent states of those emotions. Some people are stuck in moods, because they do not have the vocabulary or awareness of their feelings. Have you ever found yourself melancholy or blue, only to later realize all the circumstances that led up to that mood? Imagine experiencing personal loss or having a big change at work. Without realizing the impact this is having on you, you get angry at people close to you, adding to the vicious cycle of emotional chaos.

I want to break down what happens in your body in the process of feeling. Our body is constantly receiving and transmitting information to every cell. Depending on the stimuli, you may increase your heart rate, slow your breathing, blush, or feel butterflies in your stomach. This information is streamed throughout your body to your heart, nervous system, and stomach. When you are sad, you might experience a lump in your throat. When you're angry, there may be tension in your neck. When anxious, you might have sweaty palms. All of this is translated energetically into emotions, raw data translated through your awareness into your mind as you name that emotion—fear, anger, despair, sadness, etc.

When you are unaware of this internal process, you may not recognize the physiologic changes in your body are emotional indicators. This is when you say something out of character, have negative self-talk, or act out to release the build-up. Without the vocabulary for feelings—sadness, anger, despair, disappointment—you have to act them out to release the feeling.

Many addictions, especially food addiction, begin with emotions that have been stored up without acknowledgement. Research has found there is great value in actually naming your feelings. Dr. Aron Barbey, head of the Decision Neuroscience Laboratory at the University of Illinois, found that naming your emotions helps provide time to consider the emotion and its impact. Additional researchers found that by naming the feeling, you can calm the amygdala (your primitive center for fear) and reduce the reactivity. This is the equivalent to counting to five. When you can engage your cognitive brain to understand your emotions, you can identify what you are feeling and what to do about it.

With so much negative conditioning about emotions, it is not a surprise some people lack the vocabulary and awareness of their emotions. Without the ability to feel and name emotions, emotions can become toxic and disruptive. Add in chronic stress with the typical response of shutting down and going numb, you disconnect from your body, mind, heart, and soul. Soon, this becomes your new normal. This is the insidious nature of burnout.

Emotions, by their design, flow. Too often, emotions get stuck in mood states or are repressed, causing physical illness. We laid out a pathway for you to tune in to yourself and to listen to what your being wants you to know. You can start anywhere along the continuum, making sure you address every aspect.

**Body → Emotions/Feelings → Thoughts → Behavior**

Ask yourself these questions: *What am I feeling? Why am I feeling this? Is this feeling relevant to what is happening right now, or is it based in the past?*

Emotions are like the warning lights on the dashboard of your car: once they light up, you are supposed to take some action (or choose not to react) to keep your car running well. This is a good analogy, because if you ignore the warnings, your car will break down. When you *choose* not to act on your emotions, you have acknowledged them and recognize they may not be relevant to the current situation. When you ignore your feelings (maybe out of habit or fear), you run the risk of being caught off-guard by your emotions.

Use this simple flow chart above; go through the steps to build emotional awareness.

## WHEN EMOTIONS DOMINATE

It does take time, practice, and awareness to express just the right amount of emotion. It is a process that will continue to evolve as you go through different life experiences and challenges professionally. Know that emotions are hardwired into your nervous system and, according to Damasio, renowned neurologist, emotions are "action-requiring programs." This means their job is to inform you and guide you to take action. Emotions frequently get stuck in repetitive loops or mood states. The single greatest way to accelerate change is to get help from a coach or counselor. Not only will you unhook from the repetitive pattern, but you will also gain insight and grow much quicker in the process. I have worked with thousands of people helping them move beyond their emotional barriers. Check the back of the book for my contact information.

# CHAPTER 8

# EMOTIONS AS GUIDES: WHAT THEY ARE TRYING TO TELL YOU

Emotions are hardwired and part of our survival instincts. We talked about the limbic system and the amygdala, structures in the brain that are geared to instinctively (without thought) react to people, places, and situations that trigger fear. Because emotions are primal, meaning they are deep and beneath the surface, they can surprise even the most aware. Is this why exploring one's emotions is so hard for some people? When there is no attention paid to thoughts and feelings, emotions bottleneck and show up in moods. Have you ever said, "I got up on the wrong side of the bed today"? This is a general statement that can mean several things like, "Beware, I may be irritable. Just letting you know; don't take it personally."

If emotions are instructive and designed to inform us, what does this statement tell you about yourself? It implies that people steer clear of you because you are not yourself and sends a second message that you may not be in control.

I remember a patient who complained very loudly about the "service" he was receiving as a patient. In the ICU, this was a clear indication they were feeling well enough to be transferred to a less acute unit. I wanted to satisfy this patient, and, thinking I was doing the right thing, I approached him in a kind and caring voice and said, "Sir, you seem to be angry. How can I help you?"

People down the hall could hear the eruption and came running as he screamed, "I am not angry!" Ever had that happen?

I learned that just because I was aware of his anger, that didn't mean that he was. It is not a good idea to point out a feeling or emotion that someone has completely denied. You know the saying, "Denial is not the river in Egypt." It is a powerful defense against feeling or experiencing whatever is going on in your internal world. When feelings are denied and someone brings it up to you, it is like having cold water splashed in your face to awaken you.

I was sensitive to emotions, but I was not sensitive to how other people were experiencing theirs. I tried to bridge the disconnection with this patient in a logical way and stated what was obvious *to me*. Another way to handle that situation would be to tiptoe around it: "I can see that you would like to tell me something. I am listening." When someone is angry and doesn't acknowledge the anger, the conversation is going to be uncomfortable because they are going to act out whatever they are feeling since they lack the language to express it in a healthy way.

Emotions are powerful when acknowledged and used to choose thoughts and behaviors that will achieve your goals. Emotions can also be very destructive when left unnamed and ignored. Spend time reflecting and getting to know your own internal landscape.

If the angry person is a coworker and you are confronted with their anger, you can simply say, "I will come back when you are able to continue the conversation." Even if that person does not recognize their own anger, you can read it loud and clear and set boundaries for yourself. Since you are familiar with the power of emotions and their message, you can do so with love or at least confidence in yourself to set the limits you need. I will talk more about anger soon.

So far, we have learned that emotions are hardwired and serve a purpose, but they are also influenced by what is happening "out there" in the world around us. These signals are interpreted through the filter and lens of our previous experiences, the influence of culture, our early childhood conditioning, our level of stress, our physiology, and especially our diet and lifestyle. Emotions provide information, and the more you tune in to what you are feeling, the quicker and more effective you will be at managing your emotions and mastering your mindset. This is the essence of emotional intelligence: knowing what you are feeling, and then doing something positive with your feelings.

When you lack awareness of your "bodytalk" (the physiology of your body communicating within itself), you are unaware of emotions, cannot name the feeling, and your thoughts become distorted, which ultimately also sabotages behavior. If you want to change behavior, improve performance, and succeed in your goals, you have to get down to the basics of your emotions.

## SADNESS: LEARNING TO LET GO

*"I do believe that if you haven't learnt about sadness, you cannot appreciate happiness."*
—Nana Mouskouri

Camille is a Loan Officer who found herself out of a job during the recent economic downturn. As the real estate market changed, so did opportunities for her to continue in this lucrative business. She was filled with sadness realizing she was losing a lifestyle, many good friends and colleagues, and her status as a competent professional in the banking industry.

Camille was forced to slow down and process the many losses brought about by losing her job. She had grown attached to the lifestyle she led and felt vulnerable as she thought about venturing back into her social network without the lifestyle perks.

She had many years in this industry and had quite a reputation for being competent; going back into the job market left her feeling insecure and unsure of herself. As she processed her feelings, she was able to cry, releasing her fears and learning to relax. She had a new opportunity to live life without the attachments that had actually limited her in some ways. She was free now to express her creativity and follow her instincts to create a new life.

Rosemary, on the other hand, did not move through her sadness and instead got stuck in anger. She ignored sadness's call to slow down, reflect, and review her life. She was not ready to live her life differently and ended up in a cycle of anger at the unfairness of it all.

Sadness is not the same as depression, although it is frequently associated with it. We are not going to go into detail in this book about depression. Depression is a more complex experience. There are the clinical definitions and descriptions of depression—bipolar disorder, postpartum depression, dysthymia, mild depression, atypical depression, and major depression. Many argue depression is a chemical imbalance and deny any relationship to thoughts, feelings, emotions, and their impact on this experience. As we have spelled out so far, it takes your mind, body, heart, and soul to make up feelings, moods, and thoughts. Having a plan for your depression that embraces these four elements will enable a full recovery.

Sadness is not the same as grief. Grief shows up in response to losses that are irretrievable. Grief can happen as a result of a physical death or the death of a dream, an opportunity, a period in your life, part of your body—any loss that is gone forever. There are stages of grief, and, as with all emotions, it is best to move through grief present and mindful to what you are experiencing. If your body feels heavy, your mind is slow, and it feels as though your heart is breaking, remind yourself this is part of the process. Using a journal to write out what you are experiencing will release feelings and emotions and focus your thoughts on the good that exists. Talking with someone who will listen will also help you acknowledge what you feel and keep you from feeling so alone. I highly recommend having help in moving through grief because one loss often can trigger every other loss you have experienced, and it quickly can feel overwhelming.

When sadness is not acknowledged and is ignored, you can move into despair, which is a mood and lacks the natural flow built into sadness. Crying can often provide the relief needed to let go, and, with the release of tension, you can relax and begin to restore yourself. You have heard the sayings, "I just need a good cry," or, "Have a good cry, and you will feel better." This wisdom speaks to the cleansing and refreshing nature of moving through sadness.

Sadness, with its heaviness, the desire to withdraw, and the need to cry, is a cue you need time to reflect, review your life, and let go of things that are not working. Sadness gives you a window into what you value, this helps you better understand yourself. When you can acknowledge your own sadness, it will increase your ability to demonstrate empathy. By acknowledging sadness and moving through it, you develop courage and the ability to do other difficult things. Sadness is like other emotions and is designed to flow. Acknowledge it, and remind yourself, "This too shall pass."

Acknowledging your emotions and feelings is your way out of the chaos of overwhelm and the destruction of chronic stress and into a life of abundance and joy. As we have laid out, when you ignore cues from your body and feelings which distort thoughts and behavior, you are at risk for poor decisions and other consequences of rogue emotions. It is the intention of this book and online program to "Super Self-Empower" you to move out of this cycle and heal.

In the online program and live events, we teach you mindfulness, tapping, visualization, and reframing, along with other tools to master self-awareness and release the pain of stored up emotion.

## REFLECTION

1. *When sadness shows up in your life, what do you do? How do you handle it?*
2. *How do you know you are sad? What do you feel in your body?*
3. *What happens as a result of experiencing sadness?*
4. *Have you gotten stuck in sadness? How does this interfere with your goal?*
5. *What do you need to let go of that is no longer working for you?*
6. *Do you allow the time to mourn losses?*
7. *Do you have a ritual to support the letting go process?*
8. *How do you rejuvenate yourself?*

## ANGER: THE NEED FOR BOUNDARIES

*"Anger is an acid that can do more harm to the vessel in which it is stored than to anything on which it is poured."*
—*Mark Twain*

In the movie *Analyze This* with Billy Crystal as the psychiatrist for the mobster played by Robert De Niro, there is a scene that is one of the best two-minute demonstrations on the difference between anger and rage. Billy Crystal is essentially kidnapped by the mobster, Robert De Niro, when the mobster starts having panic attacks. At one point in the hotel, Billy says, "I think you need to get in touch with your anger." Robert De Niro says, "Anger? You want me to get in touch with my anger? Okay, you want me to get in touch with my anger? You mean like this?" And he pulls out his gun and shoots the chair, ripping it to shreds. Billy Crystal is sitting on the sofa wide-eyed and stunned.

The entire movie is a great spoof on getting in touch with feelings, and I highly recommend it for its entertainment. The scene I just mentioned really highlights the incredible risk of "getting in touch with your anger."

The scene was a depiction of rage, which is frequently confused with anger. What was also significant in that clip was how fast one can lose control in the face of anger or rage and the individual differences in how anger is defined. In my practice, rarely did any of my clients see anger as a valuable emotion. People either acted it "out" with verbal or physical abuse, bullying, or yelling and acting it "in" with ulcers, heart disease, depression, addiction, or self-harm. Few people know how to express their anger.

Anger is an emotion that can quickly de-stabilize the individual and the people around them.

Anger is an important emotion. I want you to get to know and make friends with your own anger. Remembering that all emotions are designed to flow and to inform, anger alerts you to set boundaries and facilitate change. That could be simply putting your hand up and saying, "Stop," when someone is attempting to force you to do something you do not want to do or talking at you and disrespecting your space.

Are you awake to signs of anger in yourself?

1. Start with your body (physiology): where in your body do you feel your anger?
2. Next, are there other emotions associated with your anger? Do you feel powerless?

3. Now, pay attention to your thoughts, your self-talk, and your attitude toward others.
4. Finally, what is your behavior? Is this when you reach for the cake, bread, fries, or wine? When you go shopping or yell at your spouse and children? Or, do you shut down?
5. Ask yourself, "What action do I need to take in this situation? How can my anger facilitate change?"

Anger is a universal emotion that has a variety of styles of expression across different cultures, families, and genders. Women are more than likely taught to hold it in, while men are taught to express it. Some people see anger as a masculine emotion.

Grab your journal, and take a moment to reflect on these questions:

1. How was anger expressed in your family?
2. What did you learn about anger?
3. Do you express or suppress your own anger?

If your belief system requires you to "always be nice" instead of setting boundaries, you might smile awkwardly, turn red, and make an excuse for the person's behavior. Meanwhile, you have given that person permission to cross your boundaries, and you have internalized the anger instead of learning from it and flowing to the next emotion. Stored anger can fester and possibly turn into rage, shame, or hatred, along with inflammation in the body, especially the heart. When you allow your anger to become stagnant or stuck, your blood pressure rises, your heart beats faster, and a cascade of messenger molecules are released in your body setting up an inflammatory response, which we know today to be the source of heart disease. You may have negative self-talk or get locked into a worry cycle as you replay the event over and over as a result of anger that has gotten stuck.

When anger shows up excessively, you have a rage problem. If you argue with the TV, think there should be a law against or for something, or you explode whenever someone disagrees with you, anger has become your default emotion. Anger can give one a false impression of strength or feeling of confidence; the repetitive anger loop is actually a sign of powerlessness. The emotion of anger is not the problem; it is your relationship with anger that needs to change. When anger is heeded, it will propel you to take action and, in doing so, build a true confidence.

You may want to seek help from a counselor, therapist, or coach if you struggle with rage. I like to use a variety of approaches to quickly eliminate the emotional charge that is underneath the rage. The function of anger is to help you set limits and boundaries with people. If you are prone to rage, your boundaries are loose or nonexistent.

*What limits do you need to set in your life?*


## MYTHS RELATED TO ANGER

*Anger is a negative emotion, and it is a sign of weakness to get angry.*

> No. Emotions are designed to inform you, flow freely, and resolve naturally when you tune in to their messages. That statement reflects a distorted relationship with anger and sets you up for potential explosiveness.

*Venting anger or deliberately expressing it by hitting pillows, swearing, or yelling is a healthy way to release anger.*

> No. Research is now showing that this can escalate the anger rather than serve to release it. Engaging in mindfulness and heart-focused breathing can be helpful to slow down your response time and allow you the chance to

name your feeling, evaluate it for its relevance to the situation, and then take action.

*If I do not acknowledge my anger, it will go away.*

"Out of sight, out of mind" works in many instances; however, with emotions, what you do not acknowledge will show up later in some way. Specifically, anger can show up in passive-aggressive ways reflecting your ambivalence and discomfort with anger. Emotions are energy in motion and need to be expressed in some way.

*Showing anger gives everyone the impression I am serious about the issue. They will take me more seriously if I show my anger.*

Banging fists on the table, shouting, or issuing threats is not a sign of strength, power, or influence. It serves to shut people down, and it activates the stress reaction in you, shutting down quality thinking and creative problem-solving, interrupting listening, and interfering with good communication.

## ASSERTIVENESS OR ANGER?

The difference between assertive behavior and aggressive behavior is in how it makes the other person *feel*. Being assertive and stating your position clearly and firmly, with respect and inclusive of the other person, differs from an aggressive style that is demeaning and alienates others.

An assertive attitude is win-win. An aggressive attitude is win-lose.

If you tend to defer to others and need help practicing assertive behavior, do so in front of the mirror or on a video to become more comfortable standing up for yourself. If you tend to be aggressive, work on leaning in and practice active listening.

## REFLECTION

1. *How do you know you are angry? What do you feel in your body?*
2. *What happens as a result of experiencing anger?*
3. *How does it interfere with your goal?*
4. *How would you prefer to experience anger?*
5. *Who or what flips your anger switch on?*

## TIP: "WHITE LIGHT" BREATHING

This practice is going to help you center and ground yourself. Make sure you won't be disturbed for about fifteen minutes. Sit in a chair with your feet firmly on the floor. Tune in to where you feel your center. Breathe in and out through this center.

Take a few deep, cleansing breaths. Close your eyes, and let yourself release tension. Feel the support of the chair. Your body will feel heavy.

Imagine yourself surrounded by a beautiful white light coming in from the heavens and going into the top of your head. Imagine streams of light coming out of your feet like roots going deep into the earth—deep and wide. Continue to breathe, and feel the comfort from this solid and stable connection.

This audio and others are available in the online program, wwwhealprogram.com.

# BOUNDARIES: WHERE DO YOU BEGIN AND END?

*"I try so hard to be nice. I have listened to her problems for twenty years, and nothing changes. I make time for my mother any time she calls, and she is still lonely. What am I doing wrong?"*
—Lucy

*5:30 a.m.*

The alarm goes off. Still tired from too little sleep, Lucy dreads the day. She agreed to come into work on her day off to help out the Charge Nurse. She remembers the conversation.

"Lucy, we have a staffing crunch with Monika sick and two people on vacation, and I need someone for day shift tomorrow. You are always so dependable; I just knew you would get us out of this problem. Can you work Tuesday? I know it is your day off, but we really need you."

While Lucy agrees, she knows she was supposed to fix brownies for her daughter's play and sew her costume on Tuesday. Deep down inside, she is aware of feeling good that she is needed.

As Lucy gets in the shower, she thinks about the visit with her good friend, Teresa, who stopped by last evening unannounced. Teresa is going through a breakup, and she needed to talk. Lucy offered her wine and made her a light dinner because Teresa had said she had not eaten. Lucy pushed aside the nagging resentment that comes up when Teresa shows up. It is a one-sided relationship. *After all, she needs me*, Lucy told herself. Teresa knew Lucy was working today and stayed late anyway. She told Lucy, "I just need someone to talk to." In the back of Lucy's mind, she remembers being there for Teresa at every one of her five breakups in the last year. *But who's counting?* Lucy told herself.

*6:00 a.m.*

Lucy continues to ruminate about her mother's phone call last week when she started another guilt trip. "Lucy, you never bring the girls by anymore. Don't you love your mother?" Lucy starts to get angry and then quickly reminds herself that it must be tough living alone since her mother lost her husband. Though, her parents divorced when Lucy was eight, and her mother lived alone for over twenty years and did fine. Lucy dismisses that thought.

Lucy makes her daughters' lunches and, in the process, inhales three cookies and shoves half of a sandwich down her throat. *One of these days, I have to sit down and eat. I know this is why I can't lose weight. I hate being fat.* Ignoring the sadness that wells up when Lucy remembers herself just a year ago at her ideal weight, she moves on, grabs her coffee, and shouts to her husband, "I am leaving! Lunches are on the counter, and the girls have to be at school by 7:30."

*6:30 a.m.*

In the car, Lucy thinks about the day and remembers she is working with Pat. Pat is someone Lucy has admired because she is able to say *no* and stand up for herself. Pat went through a divorce and, as a result, went to counseling. Pat told her it was the best thing that happened to her because she learned to tune in to herself and recognize she needed to take care of herself in order to take care of other people. Pat was always talking about boundaries. *I have no idea what Pat means. What are boundaries?*

Can you relate to Lucy? Do you try hard to "be nice" while you compromise your own interests? As mentioned in the previous section, anger's message is to set limits and boundaries. You have to be aware of what you are feeling in order to take action. Lucy lives in tune with everyone else's needs and ignores her own. She tries hard to be helpful, and yet, her life just isn't working. She is overweight, in emotional pain, and ends up feeling like she failed even after all her efforts. Lucy is spending all of her energy fixing other people's problems, pleasing everyone but herself, and being nice out of fear she will upset someone.

Setting boundaries can be a tough lesson, especially if the following questions are running in the background:

1. Can I set limits and still be a nice person?
2. What if my limits make it hard on someone else?
3. Is it selfish to set limits?
4. If I am supposed to set limits, why do I feel so guilty?

Boundaries are easy to spot in the physical world: people put up fences, close the door, pull down the shades, and define their own spaces. Your body uses its proprioceptive system to note its position in space, and you move through your environment as a result of this system. This is the equivalent of your aura and extends out an arm's length around your body. Different cultures have different limits when it comes to personal space.

It is harder to set the intangible emotional and spiritual boundaries. This is especially challenging when you are not tuned in to your emotions. Boundaries define what is you and not you. Boundaries define what you are responsible for and what you are *not* responsible for. This gives you freedom to know exactly what you have to take care of and what someone else's responsibility is. You are not responsible for other people, even when they try to manipulate or guilt you into believing you are. The guilt and manipulation works because you are out of touch with your own feelings and your emotional GPS (guide to personal success).

Boundaries are also about what you will let into your life as much as they are about what you limit in your life. Are you so tuned in to others you cannot allow yourself the time and energy to tend to your interests and needs? Learning to say *yes* in your life is also part of boundaries. *What have you been denying yourself because it is so hard to say yes?*

Let's answer the above questions. Setting limits makes you a nice person, as you are recognizing where you begin and end, giving everyone the same integrity. When you take over others' responsibility for themselves, you are depriving them of the opportunity to grow. Second, your boundaries are all about you and no one else. If someone complains about your limits, it is an attempt to manipulate or guilt you into doing what they want you to do. Third, it is not selfish to set limits when your internal GPS is sending out signals (anger) to take some type of action. To be caring and loving to others means you are responsible *to* them and not *for* them; helping someone with something they cannot do for themselves is different than being responsible for someone and doing things they can do for themselves. If you constantly say yes to various demands from others, the person asking is not going to look for alternatives.

Boundaries are your way to know what is yours to take care of and what is best cared for by someone else. Just like a fence that has a gate, boundaries are meant to open and close. Boundaries are not a rigid structure like a wall, just as they are not made of sand and permeable to any pressure. It takes practice to set boundaries.

Begin with awareness of your feelings. They will let you know when someone is crossing the line. Remember, Lucy was resentful and felt sad when she remembered her ideal weight. Sadness is about letting go of something that is not working anyway. Being all things to all people was not working in Lucy's life. Making the decision to take care of herself and lose weight could be a turning point for Lucy as she lets go of this focus on what other people need and tune in to what she needs.

## WAYS YOU CAN SET BOUNDARIES

*Words are ways you set limits.* Saying no lets people know your limits. You have to say *no* more in order to say *yes* to things you want in your life.

Susan has trouble saying no. Her whole life was falling apart because of it. Susan's husband injured his back and was out of work. To be able to help him, she went on night shift. Susan was working on a promotion, and going off of days could interfere with her chances. The management team wanted to evaluate her for the position. They understood she wanted to take care of her husband and agreed to give her six weeks before making the final decision. Susan helped her husband through the surgery and the recovery and saw him progress. He was walking and able to take care of himself. She told him she was going back to day shift, and she was going for the promotion. He became furious that she would leave him now when he still needed her.

Susan was furious in return. *How could he expect me to give up even more after all I have done for him?* Susan knew to stay and continue to take care of her husband would mean she would lose out on the promotion. She kept thinking, *Who knows when another chance will come around?* She also knew that to continue to tend to her husband would enable him, and, as a nurse, she knew he was recovered and capable of taking care of himself. He was really enjoying all of this special attention. He was out of touch with his own needs and saw Susan as his answer to fill these needs.

CONSEQUENCES: some people put up "No Trespassing" signs to ensure other people stay off their property. There can be legal consequences if you trespass.

What are the consequences if someone trespasses on your emotional boundaries? It is important to stick to your guns when you set limits. *Next time you come home drunk, or raise your hand to me, or [fill in the blank], I will leave until you get treatment.*

Setting boundaries is much more fluid when you are in touch with your emotions and listen to their guidance. Trusting your intuition, respecting your anger, and learning to relax so you can tune in will help you set and hold your boundaries. Being able to define where you stop and someone else begins keeps you from taking on someone else's emotions.

Anger and shame can help you set a boundary that is neither too far out nor too limiting. Fear, anxiety, and worry can keep your boundary so tight around you that it restricts your life. As you learn to ground yourself, relax, and become more present to your emotions and feelings, setting boundaries becomes more natural.

DISTANCE, PHYSICAL AND EMOTIONAL: separating yourself from difficult of hurtful situations or people is necessary to get perspective and get in touch with yourself. You do not need stay in potentially abusive situations. Leaving the room or moving out of town are examples of physical distance, just as taking time off from relationships that are causing pain will be a way to gain a new perspective as you protect yourself.

The following self-check is adapted from Charles Whitfield, MD, and his book, *Boundaries and Relationships: Knowing, Protecting, and Enjoying the Self.*

Rate yourself on the following statements using the "1-to-10" scale, one being *never* and ten being *always*.

1. It is hard for me to make a decision.
2. It is hard to look people in the eye.
3. It is hard to take care of myself.
4. I take care of others and have little left for myself.
5. I am embarrassed and feel different from other people.
6. I do not spend time alone.
7. I cannot keep secrets.

The higher the score, the more difficulty you have in setting boundaries.

Question 1 speaks to the intrusion of other people's beliefs, thoughts, and feelings into their own and the difficulty in knowing what they really prefer.

Question 2 is about feeing bad about who you are, worried others can see right through you. When you have healthy boundaries and feel good about yourself, you can look people in the eye and not worry about getting lost or being seen for who you are. See the chapter on the Imposter Syndrome.

Questions 3 and 4 are about other people taking up so much space in your own emotional space, there is no room for your own needs. You now find your sense of accomplishment through caretaking others.

Question 5 speaks to the loss of boundaries in defining who you are. When one becomes enmeshed with others, your own uniqueness can feel wrong or bad.

Question 6 speaks to being out of touch with yourself and your inner-life. When you are spending your time and energy looking outside of yourself, it is the equivalent of rejecting yourself. When you do finally spend time alone, you may be overwhelmed with critical self-talk and emotions.

Question 7 relates to an all-or-nothing approach to communicating what is going on. You may have had early messaging about not telling anyone anything about what you feel and experienced toxic secrets in your life, so telling everything is your way to balance.

Setting and maintaining boundaries becomes easier as you learn to acknowledge your emotions and listen to their wisdom.

## SHAME: THE WOUNDING OF THE SOUL

*"Shame is a soul-eating emotion."*
—C.G. Jung

In this section, we are going to talk about the message of healthy shame and guilt, along with the destruction caused by toxic shame. This can be a difficult topic; most people either act as though shame does not exist or are paralyzed by shame in every aspect of their behaviors and lives.

There have been many mixed messages related to shame. In the late 1980s, Charles Whitfield, MD, wrote in his book *Boundaries* that shame and guilt were useless emotions. He described toxic shame and made no mention of the healthy expression of shame. When I was in my internship during my graduate degree for Clinical Psychology, I was told by a Rabbi that guilt is also useless and simply depletes your energy. Now, I can see that he too was referring to the debilitating shame and guilt that comes when these emotions become toxic. Shame is the most painful of the emotions, and, because of this, I believe many avoid feeling it or talking about it. Toxic shame is underneath much of the drama that occurs in emotional roller coasters.

Shame like the other emotions has a message to be heeded. Toxic shame is also important to listen to as it will sabotage your efforts to succeed and keep you in a sabotage loop. It is important to break the silence and talk about shame.

*Take a few deep cleansing breaths. Breathe deeply, and let go of the tension. Ground yourself as you read on. Feel your feet on the floor. Be present to your body and your breath right now. Take twenty seconds, and center yourself.*

Healthy shame and guilt are natural and universal emotions. They are powerful in guiding and directing behavior, and they serve to keep all other emotions in check. Healthy shame moderates anger, jealousy, and fear. In the past when you have gone over the top with anger, do you recoil later thinking, *Did I go overboard?* Healthy shame restores boundaries as you feel remorse and make amends for behaviors that are outside of your moral code and values. To be without shame means you are out of touch with any social norms or expectations.

Guilt and shame are related. Guilt is the sense that what I did was wrong. Shame is the sense that what I did was wrong, and I am exposed in this wrongdoing. Both, when healthy, serve to correct behavior and keep you within the bounds of social and cultural norms. When responding to healthy guilt, you will work to make it right by apologizing or taking action to restore the situation. With healthy shame, you may have feelings of wanting to shrink, your face may turn red, and you might feel bad for the act, because other people know what you did. In a healthy relationship with shame, you will reset your behavior, apologize, and learn from the experience so you do not cross that line again. Healthy shame helps you recognize you are a "work in progress" rather than a finished statue with no further polishing or sculpting possible. Shame helps us all realize it is important to keep growing in order to be a better sister, brother, wife, father, leader, citizen, or human being.

Shame reminds us all there is always room to grow and become even better as a human being. Toxic shame demoralizes and judges the essence of who you are as unworthy.

These are excerpts from conversations I have had with clients that highlight toxic shame:

> "I am forty-five years old, and I went back to school for my BSN. I want to eventually become a nurse practitioner. I have a hard time relating to my classmates who are young and are supported by their families. I am a single mother, raising my daughter and working at nights. Sometimes, I

think, *Why do I bother?* I do not think I am smart enough to do this."

"My brother is gay, and I attended Gay Pride to show support for him. One of my coworkers told others what I did over the weekend. Whenever I approach my coworkers, I hear people whispering. I am sure they are wondering about me. I put my head down when I walk past; it makes me feel small. That makes me angry because I shouldn't feel this way."

"I am going through a divorce and feel so ashamed when my coworkers ask me about my husband. I feel like I failed in that marriage. I am afraid to be around any of them. If I shared my embarrassment, they might smirk or crack some sarcastic joke. I am overwhelmed with shame over the break up."

We all have the desire to "be somebody," and when this innate longing to grow, connect, become masterful, and be seen is ridiculed, rejected, or dismissed, shame rushes in to fill the vacuum. When this is experienced in the early years of growing up, the child internalizes this rejection with belief systems that fit—*I am not worthy*. As one grows, there is a lack of confidence and the once exuberant desire to "be somebody" is replaced with withdrawal and resignation.

Body language for shame includes head down, shoulders rounded, and eyes looking away for fear that someone might see the real you. Self-talk becomes harsh, critical, and hateful: *I am so stupid. How could I have done that? What is the matter with me? It's true; I will never amount to anything.*

This critical self-talk is the defense to keep the "rejected self" hidden so as to not cause any more trouble. This is the orphaned and abandoned self. When this belief system becomes the driving force in one's self-image and is not questioned or challenged, the Orphan archetype is activated, complete with feelings of isolation and difficulty in caring for self.

Remembering the growing edge of this archetype is the decision to grow beyond the debilitating feeling of shame, step out of the safe comfort zone, and make a decision to change something in your life. The first step is become aware of what triggers the shame. Awareness is the key to transformation.

*What are your triggers to that shrinking, humiliating feeling? What is your self-talk like? Are you ripping yourself to shreds before anyone else has a chance? Are you playing small in your life?*

Toxic shame is at the root of addictions, compulsions, bullying, gossip, and high drama. It is very important to heal your own in order to stop the cycle of destruction.

## REFLECTION

Grab your notebook and reflect on the following. Start with a few deep cleansing breaths, and release any tension.

1. *When do you feel small, insignificant, embarrassed, or humiliated? Write out a few instances.*
2. *Now, as you think about those examples, tune in to your body. What do you feel? Neck tightening, a lump in your throat, shoulders hunching as you try to hide? Take a few moments and write it out.*
3. *Now, tune in to your self-talk. What do you say to yourself? (Examples: I am stupid, I am fat, I am lazy . . .)*
4. *Now, go underneath the talk. What are the feelings that are there? Anger, sadness, shame, disgust, disappointment?*
5. *What shift is happening for you as a result of bringing this shame trigger into the light of day?*

*6. What loving act will you commit to shower yourself with acceptance?*

## RESOURCE: TAPPING

Because of the intense feeling associated with toxic shame, Tapping is a great tool to release the toxic emotional charge. This frees you to move beyond this feeling quickly. Rate the level of emotional pain you feel using the "1-to-10" scale, ten being the most. Find your sore spot on the left side of your chest and, rubbing that spot, say, "Even though I have had this shame and it has held me back, I completely and totally accept myself now." Repeat this three times. Then, tap on the feelings you have of the shame. Tap as you see those people and or situations that create the shame experience. Keep tapping; go through five to six rounds. Take a deep breath. Now, rate your emotional pain. Keep tapping until you reach zero.

## TIP: ESSENTIAL OILS

What do you do to love yourself? Do something that doesn't involve food or shopping. I like to use essential oils. Lavender can be very soothing, and citrus oils are uplifting. When you purchase the HEAL package, you receive the essential oil (EO) of *Pure Joy*, a lavender blend. Inhale this throughout the day, apply to pulse points, and use to refresh and rejuvenate yourself.

# FEAR, AND ANXIETY: WHAT DO I NEED TO DO?

*"One of the greatest discoveries a man makes, one of his great surprises, is to find he can do what he was afraid he couldn't do."*
—Henry Ford

In my early twenties, I knew I wanted to travel, but I was afraid to fly. I actually grew up in fear; my home life was either so quiet, it was scary, or so loud, it was terrifying. When I decided that travel was an important goal, I had to find a way to get over my fear. Call it synchronicity, because shortly after I set my new goal, I met a pilot. He wanted to take me flying in his private plane, and I declined out of fear.

He smiled and said to me one day, "It is big world out there. Are you going to continue to live in such a small way?" Wow. I love it when people say what is in their hearts. That comment struck a nerve and opened my eyes to how I was restricting myself and living small.

I decided that I wanted to face this fear, and I would learn to fly. I knew that if I could understand something, I would not be afraid. I walked into the Flight School and told the man behind the counter I wanted to learn to fly. His name was Fred. Before I could say no, we had walked to the back, and I was getting into a small plane. Buckling the seat belt, I was thinking, *What am I doing? I am not ready for this!* Fred was quite commanding, and up we went. He banked a few turns, and I began to feel nauseated. I told Fred I thought I was going to throw up, and he yelled, "You throw up in my plane, and you will never fly with me again." Suddenly, my fear of Fred replaced my fear of flying, and I swallowed hard and kept my eyes on the horizon. It was then I learned you really can overcome your fears.

*What have your fears kept you from starting or finishing in your life?*

Fear is an emotion that comes from the amygdala, hardwired to protect us from danger. It is instinctive, and the reaction happens instantaneously. The amygdala sends the trigger to the hypothalamus, which then creates the physiological patterns for that fear. Your heart rate can go up, and you might feel a lump in your throat, tension in your neck, numbness in your hands, and any number of other physical reactions. This is why I suggest you tune in to your body and follow the flow—**Body → Emotion/Feelings → Thoughts → Behavior**—to master self-awareness and learn from your body.

Fear triggers the fight-or-flight response and the stress reaction. Your amygdala is the storehouse of all your fear experiences (even those you forget) and responds immediately when it senses an experience similar to what has been stored. Most of the time, people are not aware of the origin of their fear and may not be consciously aware of it, but the amygdala will trigger physiological changes in mind and body, putting you in the fight-or-flight mode. Confronting your fears allows you to overcome the instinctive pull of this primitive reaction. Fears are usually specific to person, place, or situation and arise from feelings.

Fears can be real or imagined. It is usually the ones we imagine that cause the biggest problem. In my case, I lived life in a hyper-vigilant fear state related to early conditioning. I was afraid of new experiences and situations I could not control. Fear was not flowing or instructing me; instead, I was stuck in a fear state, which got the best of me at times and limited my experiences.

At different points in my life, I woke up and faced my fears. I allowed fear to instruct me to take action and do something different. Once I stopped resisting and faced the fear, I awakened to a broader view of myself and deeper connection to my innate wisdom. As a result of embracing the unlimited possibilities inherent in my intuition, I developed a very keen insight. This enables me to zero in on my clients' issues and target the problem, and, using the power tools of transformation like Tapping and visualization, they can quickly release the barriers to their goals. After seeing the rapid and lasting change that can happen over and over in thousands of people, I am convinced infinite potential exists when your deepen your connection with yourself and learn to communicate with heart, mind, body, and soul.

Fear, when chronic and generalized, becomes anxiety. Anxiety arises from thoughts. It can catch you in an endless thought loop: *Did I sign off on that contract? Did I forget something? What if xyz happens, what then?* And on and on and on. Many people I talk to experience this type of endless questioning at the close of their day. Anxiety, when not chronic, can serve as a messenger helping you clarify a situation in your life and take action.

I had a client who came to me for sudden onset of a bridge phobia. There were several bridges, including the large Chesapeake Bay Bridge, to cross when going from the eastern to western shore. Terry was a Regional Director of Nurses for a home health agency and frequently traveled to both shores. She had not had any previous trouble or anxiety crossing the bridge. She came to me because she heard my approach worked quickly.

When I asked Terry to describe what was going on in her life at the time, she mentioned she had just turned fifty-five. She had a party at work, but several people had not come that she had expected to celebrate with her. Later, she found out that a new local manager threw a party, and several of her close friends went. She was on the phone crossing the bridge when she found that out. Terry was very focused and known for her ability to stay calm. Terry routinely ignored her feelings and did not make the association between her distress at learning this news and crossing the bridge. Terry had put it out of her mind by the time she crossed the bridge, focused instead on the pressing issues facing the agency. It was a week later when the bridge phobia started.

I used Tapping to quickly eliminate the feelings of fear and the stress reaction, enabling Terry to feel calm when she thought about the bridge and the phone call with her coworker. She was able to recognize her feelings of inadequacy and insecurity that came up as a result of the birthday party. Turning fifty-five recently brought up thoughts of feeling old and not able to compete with her younger managers. Tapping and reframing worked to help Terry understand that fearful and anxious thoughts are exaggerated, and, while they can be instructive, it isn't useful to take these thoughts literally. Her anxiety was her cue to re-evaluate her strengths and value as an experienced leader, as opposed to reacting to the fears that she was "too old." Terry and I had one session. She called the next week so excited that not only could she drive on the bridges without any anxiety, but she also had "gotten her mojo back" and felt strong and confident as a leader. It would have been ideal to continue to work with Terry to help her relate better to her emotions. However, she saw this quick fix as "enough" and did not come back for another session.

When anxiety becomes chronic, it can be the body's way of avoiding something. Chronic anxiety shrinks your world in the effort to avoid feeling the anxiety. It was great that Terry decided to face this phobia and get beyond it, rather than changing her lifestyle to accommodate the fears.

*How do you handle anxiety? Is there a message for you in this anxiety?*

Anxiety, as part of the fear emotion, wants you to take some action. Much of the anxiety people experience can be the result of the constant state of distractions and not being able to remember what they did. Use your phone to create lists or download one of the many apps that will help you stay organized. You may want to question your anxiety and ask why you are feeling it and what triggers the feeling.

## INSTINCTS AND INTUITION

Instincts are natural tendencies to behave in a certain way. Birds know when to fly south or north and how to build a nest to protect their young. Animals have instincts that warn them of danger and when things are safe. I have talked about the survival instinct and the stress reaction that causes so much distraction today because survival is not really being threatened. This is the strongest instinct we have, to survive. This is also the instinct to grow and develop. Scientists have found that instinctive behavior is hardwired into every cell; from birth, the single cell divides and grows based on the blueprint that is written into that cell.

Instincts can develop based on emotions that get triggered. If you grew up in a chaotic home, you may develop a keen awareness so you can read facial expressions to know when the next eruption is going to take place so you can avoid it. This ability to notice nuances in people is later regarded as one of your strengths when you have to manage people and provide guidance.

Very often, when working as a nurse in the critical care units, I would have an instinct when someone would code and have a medical emergency. Instincts come from the inside and are reflected in a gut feeling that you just know something. It can show up as a persistent thought or a hunch. Way too often, instincts get lost in the noise of the day-to-day grind, drowning out the intelligence in this innate wisdom.

*Are you open to your instincts?*

Intuition is the capacity to read the instincts that come from body-mind messages. We talked about how your body is constantly sending and receiving information about everything you experience. The body scan practice to tune in to your "body talk" will help you interpret your feelings, thoughts, and emotions. And as HEAL points out, your emotions reflect what might be out of balance. Intuition, also called the "sixth sense," is the result of perceiving beyond your five senses, independent of your reasoning skills. It is something you just know to be true.

Caregivers frequently use their intuition as they take care of their patients. In her book *From Novice to Expert*, Patricia Benner writes about the blending of intuition with clinical judgment to manage complex clinical data. When responsibilities increase, it is important to quiet yourself and activate resilience to support healthy emotional engagement and intuitive intelligence. Mona Lisa Schulz, MD, PhD, medical intuitive and author of *Awakening Intuition: Using Your Mind-Body Network for Insight and Healing*, also writes about nurses' intuition and the ability to discern what is really significant with their patients in the midst of alarms, noise, and other distractions.

The word *intuition* is derived from the Latin word *intueri*, meaning *to look within*. It is an instinct perceived by the body, mind, heart, and soul. The more you respect and honor your intuition, the more it reveals to you. Unfortunately, many do not trust their intuition and rely on concrete evidence to support their hunches. How many times have you said, "I wish I would have listened to my intuition"?

*On a scale of one to ten, ten being always, how much do you trust your intuition?*

Intuition is part of a larger conversation you have with your emotions, your bodily sensations, and your thoughts and feelings. Learning to trust your intuition will help you take back your personal power for more satisfying relationships.

## TIP: DEVELOP YOUR INTUITION

Here are a few steps to develop your intuition. Intuition is not logic and does not follow an analytical thought process. The first step to connect more with your intuition is to *relax*.

1. Spend time quieting your mind and centering yourself. Use the grounding exercise from the Anger section.
2. Practice mindfulness. Spend time not thinking. Increase your awareness and your ability to stay present without having to think about something.
3. When relaxed and centered, ask your inner guidance for an answer to a dilemma you are having. Write down the response.
4. Follow through on your gut instincts. This helps to build trust.

## BOREDOM: THE CALL TO GO DEEPER

*"The two foes of human happiness are pain and boredom."*
—Arthur Schopenhauer

Boredom is defined as dullness of mind, lack of interest, and lack of joy. Boredom could be a reaction to feeling powerlessness or resigned to a life that is stuck. Boredom could be a way to hide out and not have to show up for life. Boredom blunts feelings and may be the impetus to search for the next thrill; the promotion, new car, next tattoo, new boyfriend, lover, piece of pie—you name it. Boredom could be the way to live life in the shallows of thrills and easy gratification, rather than going deeper into one's life in a mindful and more conscious way.

Boredom sets up a cascade of destructive behaviors like addictions to food, alcohol, and drugs; sabotage to self and the workplace; and flat and unfulfilled relationships, furthering the pattern of superficial engagement in life.

Boredom is the result of low expectations for you and your life. There is a lot of talk about stress and burnout having negative consequences and very little about the consequences of rust out—not having enough stress to motivate and stimulate you. The ideal condition for a full life is to stretch beyond your comfort zone. This is the underlying condition of the Flow state, which we will talk about soon. This is the opposite of the state of boredom, which is like being suspended, waiting.

The next time you feel bored, ask yourself, *What am I avoiding? Is boredom a holding place where I simply tread water for fear of stepping out of my comfort zone? What needs to be made conscious?*

Boredom is a mood state where the focus is on the passing of time rather than the engagement of the mind and heart with meaningful activities. Boredom is a way of being in the world, according to Heidegger, a German philosopher known for his work on *Being and Time*. He was one of the main philosophers we studied in graduate school. He described three types of boredom: being bored by something, bored with something, and a generalized boredom with life itself.

Is this an age of boredom where young people especially are disenchanted with society? Has the power of the machine or technology captivated their attention without indulging their hearts and souls in meaningful relationships?

*Do you complain about being bored? Are you bored with your job? What are you afraid to do that you long to do?*

## HAPPINESS: THE WELLBEING INDICATOR

*"Know yourself.*
*Control Your Desires.*
*Take what's yours.*
*Remember Death."*
—Jennifer Michael Hecht, *The Happiness Myth*

Happiness is a very individual experience. Thousands of years ago, Aristotle recognized that more than anything, people sought happiness. It is an experience people seek for its own sake. It can be an experience that defies words. Some people don't like the word *happiness* because it is overused, sounds like a cliché, and seems trite. I like the word because just saying it forces me to smile. I get that happiness is more than just a cheerful attitude and more than positive emotions. Life gets pretty complicated, and I think it's okay to be satisfied with happiness at any point on its elusive continuum, from being cheerful, positive, satisfied, content, purposeful, connected, in the flow, to existentially happy.

Defining happiness is tough and may be why some people start out by saying what happiness is not. It is not having all the money or time in the world. It is doing something meaningful. It is not feeling good all the time nor is it a destination. It is fleeting, elusive, and takes time. Trying too hard definitely gets in the way of happiness.

*How do you define happiness?*

Researchers say happiness is a combination of your level of satisfaction with life and how good you feel day to day. They say it depends mainly on your genetics. Hmm?

Abraham Lincoln said, "Most folks are as happy as they make up their minds to be." He should know, since he was depressed a lot during his life. He also knew he would do something big in his life and eventually brought his gift to the world, legalizing freedom for all. He may not have appeared happy and cheerful, yet he certainly used every bit of talent and each gift he had as he embraced the purpose for his life.

I understand science may want to credit genetics with the why and how of disease and behavior. However, I am sure there are thousands upon thousands of people who have defied their family gene pools and achieved true happiness. Bruce Lipton, PhD, cellular biochemist and author of *The Biology of Belief*, writes about the plasticity of genes and the influence of the environment, including your thoughts, on the expression of genes related to cancers and other devastating diseases. This includes those genes that regulate happiness.

I agree with President Lincoln: happiness is up to you.

*Are you engaging all of your talents in the pursuit of your life? What do you think is most important to be happy?*

After working with people for twenty-five years, I have found people to be most authentically happy when they are involved in meaningful activity. It is quite a balancing act and very much trial and error to find the right mix of meaning, purpose, self-control, indulgence, reflection, laughing at yourself, and going after what you want—oh, and remembering that, in the end, we can't take any of it with us. This is what the author of *The Happiness Myth*, Jennifer Hecht, talks about in her book; it is an excellent timeline chronicling philosophers, poets, and greats discussing happiness.

*Can't I just buy some happiness on Amazon.com?*

Sure, you can buy some temporary happiness, some woo-hoo, feel-good, this-makes-my-tummy-smile-and-me-look-good kind of happiness. I say, enjoy it! Many people want to discount this as shallow and not credible as happiness. How many out there have heard, "You can't buy happiness"? Most people are not buying that (oh, a pun!). Retail therapy has been quite effective in avoiding feelings of despair, disappointment, loss and regret. Many people have the debt to prove it.

Am I encouraging a shopping addiction? No, I am simply promoting being present and in charge of one's life. If buying lipstick at Sephora feels good, enjoy it. Also be aware of deeper emotions you may be avoiding by shopping. Deal with the deep emotions of sadness, regret, fear, anger and then shop. Chances are you will not buy anything.

Self-awareness helps you fine-tune your life so it matches your desires. Be present to yourself. Remember our body scan formula and tune in to what is happening in your body, what emotions show up, and the feelings, thoughts, and behaviors that follow—what is the message underneath all of this?

Happiness is a choice, a state of mind that is elusive; most people pursue it by trying to acquire things or to become something. That is okay because, somewhere along the line, many will wake up when "stuff" no longer satisfies them.

Historically, philosophers have noted that happiness comes from knowing yourself. Many current philosophers and people I know would agree. I would say that 100% of people who have entered into a coaching relationship with me all leave pleased with themselves and much happier as a result of going deeper into themselves and learning what is most important to them. They may not be happy with their lives or satisfied with where they are, but they are happy with themselves, content that they have passed through their own firestorms and come out the other side more in charge of their lives than before.

Other philosophers talk about self-control as the way to happiness. This is also agreed upon today by many people who can attest that being able to moderate their desires today enables them to enjoy more pleasure tomorrow. Overindulgence today compromises health, wealth, and the pursuit of happiness. Self-control feels good when you break away from the stranglehold of cravings that usurp your power. When you feel good, you make better decisions. Mindfulness is an approach to enjoy every moment, and it requires a presence and awareness. Overindulgence may seem like it is living in the moment, but it is dulling your appreciation of the satisfaction in the moment.

Practice savoring. This is an indulgence of your senses rather than an indulgence in something. Whether it is wine, chocolate, aromas of essential oils, lovemaking, painting, dancing, or whatever pleasure you would like to indulge, give yourself the time to experience it with all of your senses. It is an experience of quality, fullness, and complete pleasure. Savor the moment, and indulge your senses. Resist consumption.

In his 2004 book, *Authentic Happiness*, Martin Seligman says that authentic happiness can be broken into three elements: positive emotion, engagement, and meaning. This fits with what modern and ancient philosophers have said. Positive emotion may be transient; it is in combination with engagement (mustering all your talents and strengths) that builds optimism. Optimism enables one to pursue meaning and connect with the greater good; a formula for authentic happiness. This translates into showing up every day, smiling, and giving it 100% of your ability. This is a ticket to a happy life.

In his 2011 book, *Flourish*, Seligman reconstructs his theory on happiness and expands it to a theory on wellbeing. He wondered how the desire to pursue mastery and success for their own sake fit into his theory on happiness (he actually calls it positive psychology) and sought to understand it in the context of wellbeing. Depending on where along the happiness continuum you look, you can find mastery, flow, and wellbeing. We are going to discuss these shortly. Happiness can indeed be elusive if you have not defined it for yourself.

*Think about times you felt happy. Remember them all over again, and let your entire being be filled with this joy. Hold this experience in your mind's eye, letting it flood your body, mind, heart, and soul.*

There are a few things that are universally agreed upon to increase your happiness. The first is gratitude. Being thankful is engaging the language of the heart and elevates your feelings and thoughts to a bigger perspective. This is the language of your soul and spirit; this is your eternal and infinite nature that wants you to stop and smell the coffee and the roses and the perfume and wine and just have fun. Gratitude is one of the practices you can embrace to keep you in the present moment.

The other universal way to increase happiness is to give to others. For caregivers, this becomes a trap, because endless giving is the myth of the Caregiver archetype. Giving to others when done without expectation of anything in return or from a full heart is indeed rejuvenating. Not giving because you are exhausted or want to conserve your own resources doesn't block your happiness, either. Giving to others is a way to take your mind off your problems.

Practice random acts of kindness and pay it forward. I used to drive over the Chesapeake Bay Bridge frequently and, when I would get stuck in long toll lines, I occasionally paid the tolls of people behind me. It felt so good, and the act itself took little extra time and a small financial commitment. Give money to the Salvation Army. Buy a chocolate bar to support the school projects and let them keep the chocolate. In my twenty-plus years of practice, I have given free talks and free sessions. Be sure to balance giving with the ability to graciously receive. This way you will not burn out. You can only give freely what you are willing to receive.

### TIP: KEEP A GRATITUDE LIST

Keep a notebook handy and begin a Gratitude List. When you think of it, write down three to five things you are grateful for. Read through this list before you go to bed, when you are struggling to feel happy, and when you feel stressed out. This exercise has a cumulative effect, filling your heart and dramatically increasing your happiness.

# CHAPTER 9
# YOU ARE MORE THAN YOUR EMOTIONS

HEAL was written to help you increase your awareness of your emotions so you can ultimately have greater influence in your day-to-day interactions and overall success in your life. The reason emotions are so important, beyond emotional intelligence, is they block your energy field. The suggestions to be present and mindful and use your thoughts deliberately are meaningful because you are more than just a physical and emotional body.

**You are pure energy.**

Ancient mystics have always known this. Scientifically, evidence of an energy field was first mapped out in the 1940s when a researcher, Harold Burr at Yale University, found that the energy field of a salamander was actually shaped like the adult animal and *originated in the unfertilized egg*. The energy field preceded the birth of the animal! Since then, much more has been discovered about the dimensions of the human energy field.

In the early 1900s, Einstein discovered that matter and energy were interchangeable when he came out with his famous equation, $E=mc^2$. Particles were noted to be *both* a wave and a particle, and these mutually exclusive properties coexisted within the same electron. This changed how scientists viewed the relationship between energy and matter. This meant that one could convert matter into energy and also energy into matter. Matter has a complex energy field governed by its own internal intelligence, and it is this "field" or "matrix" that can be manipulated through various techniques to change your experience, physically and emotionally.

In the 1960s, there were a number of studies that looked at the effect of psychic energy on living systems. Dr. Grad from Montreal studied the effect of energy healers on the germination of barley seeds. He soaked seeds in salt water, known to retard the growth of the seed, essentially producing a sick seed. The energy healer then laid hands on a container of salt water that was to be used to germinate the seeds. The amazing results demonstrated that the plants receiving the water from the energy healers grew taller and produced more chlorophyll than the plants that did not receive this water.

The experiments became more complex. In one very intriguing variation, not only did the energy healer lay hands on the water to germinate the plant, but a group of depressed patients held the water to be used on a different set of seeds. The experiment revealed that the seeds germinated with the water held by the depressed patients actually suppressed the growth rate of the seedlings while the healer's water produced healthier plants.

Energy healing continues to be demonstrated anecdotally through personal experiences and also through scientific inquiry. The above experiments not only demonstrate the value of energy healing but also the power of the subtle energy properties of water. The human body is made up of 99% water and is capable of storing both positive and negative energies.

This makes the simple act of gratitude a power tool. When you think about your body's ability to hold and store energetic vibrations, the vibration of love and gratitude will be much more healing than holding onto the emotions of anger, resentment, or shame.

Traditional medicine (and most people) ignore the value of the energy field and see the body as a collection of parts. Drugs are the mainstay of medicine and drive treatment interventions. Drugs work on the chemistry of the body and often shut down the body's natural healing mechanism. I am not against the use of medicine to heal and treat disease. I am suggesting that a strict reliance on medication can short circuit the body's natural healing mechanisms.

As a practitioner of energy modalities for several decades, I have seen amazing shifts in people's belief systems and their overall health (and wealth) when they learn to embrace this aspect of their being—their energy field.

Your energy system is the life force that supports vibrant health. It is important to make choices, every day that support your energy field. What you eat, drink and think matter tremendously. For example, not drinking enough water, excess negativity, too much sugar, and other toxic choices will create blocks in your field. The following are examples of what you might feel when this field is blocked:

- Fatigue
- Lack of motivation
- Distorted thinking
- Disconnect from others
- Chronic physical problems not helped with traditional medicine
- Cycle of sabotage behavior

The energy body is what connects us to each other and the collective consciousness (and unconscious). This energy field is what ties the mind, body, heart, and soul together.

## CHAKRAS[1]

Chakras are composed of high-frequency energy strands. Those who can see energy would perceive these as wheels of light. The life force is channeled to the physical body and enters through the chakras. Each chakra represents emotional and spiritual wellbeing and provides the life force for health and vitality. The functions and deeper purposes of the chakra system is a vast area of study. This is a brief introduction to the chakra system and how it relates to your wellbeing.

Chakras are vortexes of energy, with the major ones running along the spine. There are minor chakras in the hands and elsewhere. Chakras govern the endocrine system. They transform energy from your aura and meridians. Each chakra governs different physical systems in the body.

Chakras can be damaged or blocked through an emotional upset such as conflict, loss, or accidents. Fear, anxiety, and stress are common causes of chakra malfunction. The disruption of the chakra and aura create disease and disturb the overall energy balance or life flow. Psychological problems may cause "blockages," obstructing the flow of energy into or out of the chakras.

---

[1] Pronounced "ch" as in church.

It is necessary to have *balance* throughout our energy system for good health and wellbeing. Emotions that get stuck, stagnant, or repressed will create blocks in this energy system. The amount of energy flowing through our chakras determines how well we function emotionally, physically, and spiritually.

It is not necessary to know everything about the chakras or energy fields in order for your energy to clear. This brief summary will help you understand the energetic development of your self-image, beliefs, and behavior. Clearing the energy field is one of the most effective methods for lasting change.

Many of my clients have said, "I have been in therapy for years, and even though I understand what happened in my childhood, nothing has changed! After the energy work, the self-sabotage stops!"

This is the value of energy work. The body remembers and stores the trauma, experiences, and memories; using energy methods to release the trauma will finally free you from the burden of that old emotional charge *and* change your behavior.

Visualization, tapping, and essential oils are the approach I use to quickly balance your chakras for greater energy flow. There are also hands-on energy techniques that will open your energy channels for greater flow.

Any time you use intention to think certain thoughts and release fears and self-doubt, you allow your energy field to flow.

Trying too hard gets in the way; use the suggestions in this program and allow the shift to happen.

## CHAKRA VISUALIZATION

Sit comfortably in a chair. Feet on the floor. Be sure to turn off your phone and have privacy so you won't be disturbed. Give yourself fifteen minutes.

Take a deep, cleansing breath and exhale. Repeat. As you take in the next breath, hold it on a count of four and exhale. As you do, close your eyes and sink into the chair. Completely relax.

Imagine roots coming from your feet going deep into the earth—deep and wide. Imagine a stream of light pouring into the top of your head. Pull in this light with your breath. You are filled with sparkling, glistening points of light that are filling your entire being.

See a string of lights running from the base of your spine to above your head. These balls of light are all rotating, creating a beautiful rainbow of red, orange, yellow, green, deep blue, purple, and the most brilliant white light edged in gold. As this light travels up, through and around you, your energy field is cleansed of doubt, negativity, fear, and disease and is now magnetized.

Breathe in and out, taking in this beautiful array of color. Let the relaxation heal you. Know that this process will continue to work all by itself for as long as is necessary.

When you are ready, open your eyes, stretch, and become completely and totally awake and alert.

Be sure to drink lots of water.

### Aura

We all have an energy field that comes from within and surrounds us. This field is made up of the multi-dimensional aspects of the electromagnetic energy within the human body and spirit. This energy field can be accessed using many of the techniques we present in this program.

### Meridians

In Chinese medicine, the channels of energy that carry the life force, *chi*, are called meridians. We will access this energy when using the rapid-release technique called *tapping*.

## SUMMARY

- Every cell in your body is surrounded by an electrical field. This becomes your field, your aura.
- This field is also in contact with the energy in the environment. This is the primary way you relate to people and your environment
- There is not a "nerve ending" for detecting energy; you sense it through color, sound, light, emotions, and intuition.
- Your emotions are most likely stuck in habitual patterns that keep you reacting the same way, attracting the same relationships and the same situations. This is why things do not seem to change. Blocked emotions disrupt the natural flow of your energy field.

- Emotions flow from conscious to unconscious to the Divine realm. Most problems with emotions happen somewhere on this continuum: mind, body, heart, and soul.
- Emotions can be your guide to shifting blocks that are limiting your relationships, career, and all aspects of your life.

The HEAL program uses power tools (amazing techniques) based in energy psychology. I have used these energy tools for decades and have seen effective results with thousands of people. You do not need to keep struggling or suffering for a "long time" because of a problem that may have happened decades ago. Energy shifts are immediate.

*Are you willing to let go of the wound, anger, or block and let your energy field clear it?*

Most traditional techniques that work on emotions deal only with the conscious and unconscious mind and do not recognize the value of using the energy field.

Energy-clearing works quickly. As you clear the old habits and patterns of reacting to your emotions, you will relate to the world and people around you in an authentic way.

# TAPPING TECHNIQUES

Tapping is one of the many techniques in energy psychology that "work" by clearing the energy field. Chinese medicine uses a meridian system with different acupressure and acupuncture techniques to optimize the flow of the life force, the *chi*.

Traditional medicine, at this point, only recognizes the energy field in diagnostics (MRI, CAT scan) and does not engage this field for any type of treatment—yet. This simple tapping technique is very effective in releasing anxiety, fears, phobias, anger, and negativity. I have included it among the Stress Strategies because I have used this with thousands of people in a variety of circumstances and have seen it work dramatically.

This energy field can become blocked and or stagnant as a result of diet, toxins, traumas, and strong emotions like chronic stress. Not drinking enough water is enough to interrupt the flow of your life force energy. As your energy field becomes blocked and weakened, you risk developing many health challenges and problems with focus, mood, concentration, and energy. Chinese medicine recognizes energy channels that move the life force—*chi*—throughout your mind, body, and spirit.

Tapping techniques (TT) use simple acupressure on points on the face and hands to release this blocked energy that can show up as fears, phobias, anxiety, negativity, headaches, tension, and so much more. Tapping has been found to work effectively on pain, nausea, and many other "physical" problems as well. Tapping is a good tool to balance your energy field for greater performance and more joy.

Tapping techniques are so simple and easy to use—we suggest you try it on everything! More than 85% of the time, it works within five minutes!

Wouldn't you like to feel more calm and centered? Many people discount the results because they don't understand *how* this could possibly work. When you turn on the lights, do you really have to know *how* this energy is moving through the wires before you flip the switch? So it is with tapping. When you tap, you may not know exactly how it works, but if you get results in five to fifteen minutes a day, does it really matter?

What you believe sets up expectations. If you think only of the worst-case scenarios, then that is what you condition yourself to expect. TT will clear your negative and limiting beliefs and the emotional overtones that support those beliefs.

*What do you spend your time predicting about your life? Which thoughts keep you stuck?*

Your belief system will activate your potential *or* hold you back. Your thoughts, beliefs, and emotions either support optimal health and success or set you up for failure and even physical disease.

What you focus on grows, so if you live in fear, then you create fear experiences. You always have a choice about what kind of movie to play in your mind as you go about your day. However, there are times when you may feel stuck or unable to change this movie. Becoming more aware of what you say to yourself or the emotional pattern with which you live is key to releasing these blocks. By using this simple, rapid-release tool, you can shift out of the negativity into a positive and empowered mindset.

We provide audio and video in the online program that take you through the tapping sequence. Tapping is very effective in releasing limiting beliefs and blocks to greater joy and peace. TT is simple and will work even if you do not believe it will. You just have to use it.

We hope you use this simple tapping technique whenever you feel anything that is distressing.

Use it as you think about the argument with your partner or coworker or friend.

Tap as you drive home from work to release any fallout from your day.

Tap before you go to bed at night to release any leftover attachments to your day.

Use it on your children as they talk about their day to help them release any distressing feelings. Tap along with them, and you will also release any stressful feelings.

## HOW TO TAP

Study the diagram on the following pages. Here is the step-by-step process for the acupressure technique:

1. Identify your fear, difficult emotion, or stressful feeling. Be as specific as you can. Note your level of distress before you begin tapping and after. Measure the emotional charge associated with the issue you chose to tap on using a scale of one to ten (ten being the worst).

2. After identifying the fear, difficult emotion, or thought, find your "sore spot" on your *left* chest area while rubbing it firmly and repeating this three times: "Even though I have 'this problem,' I deeply and completely accept myself..."

3. Then, begin tapping at the top of your head to the edge of the eyebrow, and follow the complete sequence of points on one side. While you tap, think about the stressful event, difficult conversation, or feelings that are troubling you. You can talk or stay silent; just focus on the negative feelings. This will release the intensity and help you shift out of the negative to a more relaxed and neutral place.

4. Continue tapping this sequence of points for three to four rounds, going through all the points. Stop, take a deep breath, and tune in to the emotional charge. How would you rate it now? Continue to tap until your distress reaches zero to one.

5. You may need to repeat this sequence a number of times. Persistence does pay off. You may have other emotions surface as the one you started with fades. Tune in to what you are feeling, and if it is different, make note so you can tap on that later. Stay focused on your original issue until it rates zero to one. Then, go on to the other issues that come up.

Once cleared, the problem does not usually come up again. The memory of the problem remains, but the emotional charges are gone.

# CHAPTER 10

# YOUR SUPERPOWERS

*"Every day you make choices. These daily patterns determine your success. Be your best – no matter what."*

Just because you have given up your Superhero cape, doesn't mean you do not have superpowers at your disposal at all times. So far, this book has been about tuning in to you and building awareness. This awareness is the essence of mindfulness and the foundation of success.

This reminds me of my first job as a nurse in the ICU. In nursing school, I worked as monitor tech in CCU. Never mind that is was *so* long ago when monitors did not have the recognition software they do now! I knew I wanted to work in an ICU, and, even though I was told, "That's impossible, because they do not hire new graduates to work in the ICU," I was determined. Sure enough, I was hired. Early in my orientation, I received the best advice I could get. One of the PAs on that unit noticed that I was new and nervous, and he came to me after a code and said, "Next time you see a problem, take your pulse first before you reach for the patient."

In other words, get a hold of yourself before you tackle the world. In essence, that is what this book guides you to do. Now, let's arm you with strategies you can use with your awareness for a true victory over the evil empire of stress and overwhelm.

I want to reiterate that stress and overwhelm are not emotions—they are actually the result of not naming or tuning into emotions. These Superpowers are going to help you achieve balance; feel more centered and energized in your day. Ultimately, you will have greater awareness and control over your emotions.

The Five Superpowers are:

1. The Power of Now
2. The Power of Thought
3. The Power of Focus
4. The Power of Flow
5. The Power of Love

Read through them; then engage them daily. Be deliberate as you put them into motion and you will take charge of your day. There are exercises with each super power.

## THE POWER OF NOW

*"This moment is all you really have. The past is over and the future not here yet. In this moment there is unlimited possibility."*

The point of power is in the present moment. Where do you live? In the past, replaying old arguments or scenes in your mind, or in the future, wishing and hoping for the outcome you want? Meanwhile, what has become of the present moment?

Being present has never before been so difficult. The new normal of compulsively checking emails, texts, and social media has destroyed focus and replaced it with a dazed and disengaged presence. This increases irritability and frustration. This translates into feeling more stress and tension in your body, causing more distraction. This vicious cycle is the treadmill of daily life for many people. This is the biggest energy drain today because, in the dazed and distracted zone, you make poor food choices, you make mistakes (maybe even fatal ones), and you miss out on real experiences that might boost your spirit or help you feel good. Instead, you barely remember what you're doing.

This level of distraction is complicated by your brain under the influence of the stress reaction, communicating sensations and triggers to your body and mind. . This hijacking is what distorts the present and keeps you locked into reactions. Your primitive brain likes to categorize your experiences into good, bad, right, wrong, painful, or pleasurable, and this type of thinking then dominates your rational mind. You can unhook from this by practicing mindfulness and learning to be present in the moment. This practice will expand your possibilities and release the tension, worry, and dread that comes from your primitive brain being in charge.

This superpower of now is the ability to bring your attention to the present moment and focus on what you are doing right now without judgment, or other competing thoughts. It takes practice. It is worth the effort. This is the practice of mindfulness.

Begin now.

## ATTENTION REBOOT:

Let's say you are at work in a staff meeting. You don't like being there because it takes time away from finishing up your work. In the past, to avoid feeing the resentment, your mind wandered, and you would think about your next vacation or some place you loved visiting. Since you have learned about the Superpower of Now, you want to deliberately bring your attention to the meeting. Act as if it is the very first time you have been in the meeting. What do you notice? Your only job is to observe. Let any thoughts drift away.

Use this technique with any person, place, or situation, telling yourself it is the very first time you have seen or heard or been there. Just observe and notice. What is different? This ability to reboot your attention to see more of what is around you keeps you from being complacent, smug, or stuck. It is easy to block out small details that can be quite meaningful when caught up in the "doing" of daily life. This can create an attitude of, "I know everything there is to know," or, "Nothing ever changes."

There is more opportunity around you than you realize because most people are caught up in a habit living life distracted. Bring your attention into the moment, and then learn to power up your thoughts.

# THE POWER OF THOUGHT

*"Whatever you think about, you bring about."*

It is estimated that your mind goes through 50,000 to 80,000 thoughts per day. That is between 2,000 and 3,300 per hour. Your brain weighs three pounds and has 30 billion neurons, powerhouse cells that analyze, dream, plan, remember, and process 30 billion bits of information per second. You have at your disposal a supercharged miracle that can leave even the best computer in the dust. Unfortunately, most people don't bother to turn it on and simply go through their days on autopilot.

What choices do you make during the day that are out of habit? Chronic stress quickly creates bad habits with reactive choices. For example, if you chose to get that double mocha chocolate latte, what were your thoughts? I deserve that? I feel stressed. Too often the origin of these thoughts is not identified. Let's say, it was a fight with a spouse and you may feel disappointed about something. Instead of registering that feeling and dealing with it, you get a double mocha latte. Very quickly, anytime you feel disappointed, you will end up craving something like the latte. This is now a habit.

Ninety percent of the thoughts you think are habits.

Many years ago, I had a client who was a CNO (Chief Nursing Officer). He came to me to improve his communication skills. He was seen as aloof and detached by nurses. He said that he never felt comfortable interacting with the nurses and felt all they did was complain. He shared that early in his life, his family moved around a lot. He never made good friends and felt like an outsider in school. He had not thought of that until we explored his current hesitation to interact more with the nurses. His thoughts are based on forty-year-old data of moving frequently and never feeling comfortable around people—data that is no longer relevant.

Is your supercomputer being powered by outdated and old software? Are you on autopilot? Question yourself, and ask why you are thinking or doing what you are doing. Do you really want that pie, burger, fries, (you name it)? Do you really want to drink thirty-two ounces of soda a day? Do you want to follow through with that Facebook post? What are you doing that is based on old programming?

Change your thoughts, and you will change your life. This is the single most important thing you can do to change any aspect of your life; upgrade your mindset. I grew up in a home steeped in despair and negativity. I wanted so much to go beyond the limitations my parents set for themselves. I did not have the advantages of money as we lived paycheck to paycheck, and I was determined to find a way to break out of this limiting situation. Early on, I learned that when you master your mindset, you master life. I am passionate about sharing this with you because the answer to any problem is to use your thoughts deliberately.

Whatever you set out to do begins first with a thought. Edison did not set out to create the light bulb with the idea he would fail. Henry Ford believed in his idea to create an automobile for the masses and turned down a secure lucrative position to pursue his dream. He succeeded because he was determined. He is famous for saying, "Whether you think you can or you think you can't, you are right."

Think about your own life. Think about a time you succeeded at something. What were your thoughts at the time? Now, go to a time when you failed or did not meet your goal. What were your thoughts like? Everything begins with a thought. What do you think about your life? Is this the thought you want to power your ship?

In our programs, we provide audio and video to take you through the process of visualization, intention, and relaxation. Learning to deliberately use your thoughts to create the life you really want is your ticket to emotional freedom.

*What is the most important thought you need to change in order for your life to change?*

Knowing that everything begins with a thought, start to tune in to what you are thinking. Whenever a negative or limiting thoughts shows up, immediately change it to one that is positive. If you have trouble with a person at work and tend to grumble about having to work with that person, Ugh, I really do not want to work with her; my day is shot, can become, I am open to great possibilities working with this person; I choose to shift my attitude.

Keep in mind it is easier to maintain a positive attitude than correct a negative one. Changing negative thoughts can be done, and is well worth it. After all, who do you prefer to be around—someone complaining or someone who is positive? The first step to changing your negative thoughts is to recognize you are stuck in this habit. Negativity is a habit. Keep a Thought Journal: note the day, time, what you are doing, what you have eaten, and who else is around. This will help you recognize when you feel negative and tune in to your thoughts. Are you focused on a disaster scenario or focused on a problem? Immediately shift your mind and imagine the scene as you want it to happen. What is important here is to realize you have control over what and how you think.

### THOUGHT REBOOT:

Engaging the superpower of thought is doing exactly that: taking control of your thoughts. Set up a new habit of affirmations. Use the card deck that comes with the Heal Program and sprinkle them around your home, car, or office. When you brush your teeth, get in the habit of repeating affirmations to yourself. Think of other times during the day when you intentionally focus your thoughts. This becomes your new habit. Your thoughts are influenced by your emotions. Often, changing your thoughts will shift your feelings and mood. The more you focus on the positive, the happier you will feel. Changing your thoughts is not something you do once and then forget about it. It is a process you will continue to do, and it gets easier every time you set your intention.

Thoughts come out of the unconscious part of your mind, and your conscious mind is its gatekeeper. The more self-aware (conscious) you are, the greater control you have over what you think. Being aware—using the superpower of now—you are able to protect your unconscious mind from the predators of fear, doubt, and other influences that come from people, places, and situations. Advertising on TV, radio, and the internet are constantly trying to instill an urgent need and desire for the product through emotionally charged images. The unconscious is more susceptible to suggestion during very stressful times or in heightened emotional conditions like fear and panic. Staying present rather than distracted by the stress reaction will help you keep positive thoughts front and center and the negative ones at bay.

*What are the attitude adjustments you can make to transform the outcomes in your life?*

The superpower of thought is your opportunity to change the outcome and the trajectory of your life—one thought at a time.

### THE POWER OF FOCUS

*"Success is directly related to your ability to focus."*

Focus is a superpower, a skill you can develop—possibly the most significant. In the Age of Distraction, everything is competing for our attention, and the inability to focus has become quite a disadvantage.

Do you know what is most important for you to focus on at work? Do you have priorities for your family? Are you clear on your values? Have you defined your personal goals? Getting clear takes time. I highly recommend you set aside time to think this through. When you are clear about what is important and what you need to focus on, it is easier to say no and set boundaries.

Here are a few strategies to support this *superpower of focus*.

1. Evaluate your habits. Do you have habits that are aligned with your goals? 90% of your behavior is automatic and based on habits. Too often, these habits get in your way of

performance and productivity and cost you precious time and energy. Getting derailed because you stayed up late again and now can't focus on what is in front of you is a habit you can change with this "Cost-Benefit" Analysis.

Work through it with the chart on the next page.

| Cost Benefit Analysis of Your Habits | | |
|---|---|---|
| Habit that Blocks Success | Successful Habit | Strategies to Support New Habit |
| **Procrastination**<br><br>Cost<br>1. Miss deadlines<br>2. Lose credibility<br>3. Feel overwhelmed<br>4. Miss opportunities for promotion | **Focus and Finish; Improved Follow Through**<br><br>Benefit<br>1. Greater confidence<br>2. More time to spend on planning<br>3. Seen as an effective leader and problem solver. | 1. Schedule time to read emails and texts. Reduce the distractions during the day.<br>2. Delegate the jobs that are not part of my role.<br>3. Schedule time to work on projects and limit activities that detract from their completion. |
| **Implementation Date:** July 29 | | |

2. Spend time every day unplugged. Interruptions from text, instant messages and other bells and alarms from the phone make it very difficult to focus.

Keep an Interruption Log and notice how often you interrupt yourself by checking email or social media. Distraction is a habit. Build your focus muscles.

3. Use visualization to see yourself achieving your goal. Set up fifteen to thirty minutes at the start of every day to pray, feed your spirit, read inspiration, define your priorities for the day, and visualize your goals. Visualization is detailed in the section on Stress Strategies.

4. Get the help you need. If you are crunched for time, what can you hire out so you can focus on your biggest priority? Hire a cleaning service, painter, landscaper, or other services so you can enjoy time with your family. What can you delegate and or train your assistant to do so you can focus on what really matters at work? Way too often, the reason assistants or delegation don't work is because of poor communication. You have to be clear and concise when you state your expectations.

5. Avoid the "If Only" trap. Rumination over what might happen will waste your time and drain your energy. It will dampen your desire to find creative solutions. This trap is also rooted in regrets. Work on building good habits, and you will not have to spend time focusing on what "coulda, shoulda, woulda" happened.

## THE POWER OF FLOW

*"If we agree that the bottom line of life is happiness, not success, then it makes perfect sense to say that it is the journey that counts, not reaching the destination."*
—Mihaly Csikszentmihalyi

Have you ever gotten so involved that you lose track of time and nothing else matters? This is the *superpower of flow*. This effortless concentration and enjoyment is achieved when engaged in an experience like singing in a band, playing chess or poker, golfing, dancing, skiing, reading, painting, and even working. Some people call it "being in the zone." Athletes, musicians, actors, and others talk about this experience of effortless action as the best times of their lives.

Many years ago, I worked with a physician who loved what he did, and in spite of the long hours and the demands of the job, he rarely felt exhausted. His wife was disappointed that he did not spend more time with her, and we worked on creating more balance. Since he had already learned to embrace this superpower of flow in his professional life, I helped him use this in his personal life.

What if you could create this experience deliberately?

Mihaly Csikszentmihalyi, author of *Flow: The Psychology of Optimal Experience*, writes that it is this experience of flow and not happiness that makes for an excellent life. In his research, Csikszentmihalyi found the flow experience took the individual into a different reality, opening them up to greater discovery. Flow happens when you are focused and challenged and you enjoy the experience. It does not happen when you are passively involved or disengaged. In fact, one of the best ways to get into flow is to embrace challenge.

You will achieve FLOW when you:

- ✓ Focus.
- ✓ Love what you are doing.
- ✓ Own your strengths.
- ✓ Welcome the challenge.

The opposite of flow is boredom, a state where you are not stretched and are operating below your ability. You can go from boredom to flow simply by increasing your focus and challenging yourself to learn a new skill or set a more difficult goal and enjoying the process. Flow happens when you engage yourself and stretch. Flow feels really good. It is enjoyable, and it can be cultivated. Just as you learned to deliberately bring yourself into the moment and direct your thoughts, the next step is to build in a challenge for yourself in your day. Flow requires you to invest your attention and be willing to push yourself. Success is when you meet any challenge with the same or greater response. Flow is your ticket to success. Shift your thoughts about the challenges facing you. Go after the skills you need to meet the challenge and enjoy the process.

*Are you on autopilot and just drifting through your day?*

To get into flow, you have to be willing to focus. Today more than ever, focus is a challenge. Spend time away from technology, read, or concentrate on something for twenty uninterrupted minutes. Practice the tips in this book, acknowledge and release your emotions, and always remember to breathe.

The *superpowers of Now and Thought* will help you bring yourself into the present. To engage flow, ask yourself what new things you can learn every day to make your work better. Make it a contest or experiment, and enjoy the challenge of finding solutions. Anytime you focus on the solution, you energize your confidence. When you focus on the problems, you are eroding your confidence.

## WORK REBOOT:

Practice active listening to hear what your coworkers are really saying, and avoid quick judgments and overreaction. Learn additional clinical skills, and increase your interest and enthusiasm for work. Talk with your manager to find out what expectations he or she has for your job. Express your appreciation for your manager. Take a moment, breathe deeply, and relax before you go into your patients' rooms. Be present, and let them feel you are right there with them. This mindfulness increases your observation skills and reduces their anxiety. This is a win-win.

*How will you invest your attention in your work life and increase your flow experience?*

By deliberately focusing your attention on what you can do to improve your work life (versus complaining about the job), you take charge of your thoughts and the ultimate outcome. This is operating in the superpower of Flow. The superpowers build on themselves and overlap, so the more you engage in one, the more it helps you with the others.

# THE POWER OF LOVE

*"Love is one of the most misunderstood forces in the cosmos."*
—John Randolph Price

Love is the most powerful force in the world. When you have it, you feel like the world is your oyster. When you do not have it, the world looks like your enemy. Most people end up chasing love in some form or other without realizing that they themselves are the vessel through which love flows.

I want you to be willing to allow more love in your life. This book has been about opening up to your emotions and the deeper wisdom that is available to you. It is about letting the emotions flow rather than having them bottleneck and shut down your life force. Disappointment, betrayal, and hurt takes its toll physically, mentally, and spiritually. Loving yourself is the doorway that opens you up to more love in your life from others.

Think about love as the essential life force. This life force (vibration) is the substance of everything around you. To create more of what you want in your life, the vibration of love has to flow more easily. When you shut down this vibration of energy, you limit what is possible in your life. To have more abundance in your life, you want to focus on the life-giving energy of love rather than the life-draining energy of desire.

I am not talking about the love that comes from your own personality; rather, it is the Divine Love that is the source of all creation. This Love is from God. It is the highest frequency of energy. When engaged, it changes matter, creates something new, breaks through patterns, and lifts up all consciousness.

It is hard to conceptualize. We all start out with a model of love that came from our parents or earliest experiences in family and culture. We love ourselves the way we were loved, and way too often, this is the problem. We recreate the pattern of love we received, and this pattern dictates our lives. When this pattern is inadequate, life ends up "feeling" inadequate, and the chase begins for love and happiness, thinking that things, people, or status are going to fill this longing inside.

Thinking only of protecting yourself, you might shut down from further disappointment, hurt, or betrayal. After all, being vulnerable is scary. Think back to the boundary section. Boundaries are also about what you allow into your life. Being rigid and blocking any opportunity for disappointment also shuts down the possibility for something good to happen.

Learning to listen in and honor the message of your emotions will help you to have more fluid boundaries and stay open to the *Superpower of Love*. When your heart shuts down and you disconnect from hope and the ability to forgive, you diminish the capacity to join with the Divine energy and create abundance.

You are a co-creator of your life, and *love* is what magnetizes this process.

I could go on and on writing about what love is, but to truly understand, it has to be experienced. Forgiveness, gratitude, appreciation, awe, humility, and faith are all stepping stones to opening up one's heart and soul to this universal force. Engaging the other Superpowers are going to open you to receive more love.

The first feelings of love are felt in the heart. Since ancient times, the heart center has been considered significant. This reference is not about the physical organ of the heart but rather the energy center of the heart. The heart chakra is the fourth of seven energy centers that make up your energy field. The heart has the strongest energy field of all. It is this vortex of Divine energy that serves as the center through which everything is created.

You are pure energy. It is true. The MRI, PET scan, and other diagnostic tests use the energy field to diagnose disease.

Traditional medicine does not yet use the energy field to heal. We are filled with atoms and every cell has a magnetic cell wall that contributes to our energy field. The more consciously aware you are of what you are feeling, the more you control your own field and what you attract (or not).

Think of love as the super magnet. Love heals. Think about those times when you were comforted by someone you love. Healing, wasn't it? Now, imagine Divine Love, infinitely more powerful, comforting you. This Love is available to you all the time. Ask. Be open. Receive.

*Are you open to receive love from the universe/God?*

## LOVE REBOOT:

For more love to come into your life, be willing to send more love out to others. Practice sending love to your immediate family, and imagine a circle of love surrounding them. Extend that love beyond your home to your neighbors. Practice this feeling for fifteen to twenty seconds, and work up to a minute or longer. As you practice, you will open your heart to receive more love for yourself, this enables you to give more away.

What blocks love is the old disappointment, betrayal, or heartbreak and this can be released quickly using Tapping. I have used it with thousands of people and have seen it work quickly. Tapping is effective, even if you do not believe it will work. While it is understandable to shut down, it is what keeps you from receiving the blessings that have your name on them.

Did you know the God Self within you is *you*? There is no place where God leaves off and you begin. Begin a practice of loving yourself from the depths of your *inside* to your complete *outside*. Learning to love yourself is what will ensure you live a balanced and fulfilled life. Make it a point to pour out Love to yourself and extend this to anyone with whom you have conflict, disagreement, or hurt.

Enjoy spreading love. It is the one thing that increases as you give it away. Start with yourself and you will change the world.

# LIFE IN FLOW

I hope this book opened you up to your inner wisdom. This is really the beginning of better relationships and greater possibility for your life. What will it be like to have less internal conflict? Your emotions are not the enemy, not to be feared or hated; instead to be recognized as your guide to personal success (GPS). Whether you have ignored your emotions or have been hijacked one too many times, you can begin now to tune in, identify and release whatever blocks a healthy flow of emotions.

Engage the super powers of Now, Thought, Focus, Flow and Love and transform the struggle in your day. You can change your relationships and model a new found confidence as you let go of trying too hard.

Writing this book brought together research I did in my graduate program along with what I have learned from the courageous and successful individuals I have had the privilege to work with in my private practice. It helps me fulfill my purpose to help as many people I can, live an exceptionally full life.

I hope this book supports your own healing journey. It is time to open up to your super powers and live a life that is more abundant. I will leave you with a few lines from this beautiful poem, Love after love, by Derek Walcott, Caribbean poet who won the 1992 Nobel Prize for Literature.

> "The time will come
> when, with elation…
>
> You will love again the stranger who was yourself.
> Sit. Feast on your life."

# WAYS WE CAN WORK TOGETHER

Questions? To work with me individually, you can call 1-888-71-FOCUS or email me at drh@eileadership.org. You will be amazed at quickly you move forward. Results are lasting.

Let's talk about what you may need specifically. I offer a complimentary strategy session, to schedule
**www.healprogram.com/discovery**

**KEEP IN TOUCH:**

Facebook.com/healprogram

twitter.com/drcynthiahoward

linkedin.com/in/drcynthiahoward

I look forward to hearing from you and helping you continue your journey towards healthy emotions and abundant life!

# ABOUT THE AUTHOR

**Cynthia Howard RN, CNC, PhD**, has worked with thousands of people helping them move beyond the barriers that keep them from achieving their full potential. She has specialized in the release of trauma using EMDR, Tapping and other energy tools that quickly release the emotional charge and the blocks associated with the experience.

This specialty in trauma led Dr. Cynthia to discover the secrets to breaking free of limiting beliefs and creating a life you love. She created a proven system to move people forward by releasing blocked energy and engaging the natural inclination to express oneself through imagery.

Cynthia has 10 years' direct experience in Nursing with 5 years in management roles prior to being laid off, the motivation for launching her first consulting practice. She pursued graduate degrees in psychology with the desire to understand what drives behavior. Intrigued by what motivates and inspires people to grow and develop, Cynthia has mastered many healing arts modalities including hypnosis, researched the energy field and read the works of many great philosophers.

Since 1998 through 2009, Cynthia was Director of her own wellness centers, Transform Yourself, in Maryland providing an integrative approach to well-being and high performance.

Today, Cynthia is resilience champion and the leading high performance coach in healthcare. She developed the Resilient

Leader System to support high performance leadership development. www.resilientleaderprogram.com

Dr. Cynthia is CEO, Chief Energy Officer, at Ei Leadership, the parent company that provides CE training, retreats, coaching and events. Visit www.eileadership.org

HEAL was created to provide a roadmap to individuals' inner experience so they can move through their blocks and barriers and create a truly abundant life.

# HEAL PROGRAM

*Do you feel stuck?*
*Would you like to learn how to release stored up emotions with Tapping?*
*Do you want to feel more empowered and create more of what you want in your life?*

Our HEAL program is a transformational experience. In live, online and 1:1 events you will have the opportunity to master your emotions and free yourself from the limiting beliefs that hold you back. As you increase your self-awareness you become more powerful in creating a life you really want.

Visit us online for options and information about the programs.

**www.healprogram.com**

Tune in and turn on your,

## **GPS.**

You are more than your emotions.

You are a magnificent being capable of living out your heart's desire. Begin now and live your life fully.

www.ingramcontent.com/pod-product-compliance
Lightning Source LLC
Chambersburg PA
CBHW071928290426
44110CB00013B/1519